Cold Cases:
Solved

Volume 9

18 Fascinating
True Crime Cases

Robert Keller

Please Leave Your Review of This Book at
http://bit.ly/kellerbooks

ISBN: 9798883633613

© 2024 by Robert Keller

robertkellerauthor.com

Table of Contents

Black Summer...5

Bad Obsession 13

The Gambler 19

American Nightmare...27

After the Fire...33

Have Death, Will Travel 41

Desperado...47

Storm Warning 53

Death Comes Calling 59

Rot in Hell 67

Fourteen, Going on Psycho 75

I'm the One You're Looking For 83

3,794 Days of Doubt...89

Here Comes Trouble 95

Chasing Shadows...103

Suspect Zero 111

When Hope Dies 119

The Accidental Detective 125

Black Summer

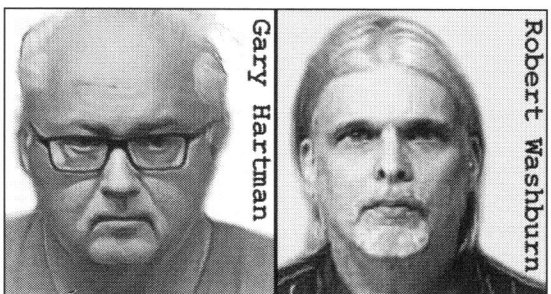

March 26, 1986, was a beautiful sunny day in Tacoma, Washington, the kind of day when kids are loath to be indoors. Sisters Michella, Angela, and Nichole Welch had their piano lessons scheduled for that afternoon but that gave them plenty of time to head to Puget Park, about two miles from their home. The girls nagged their mom, Barbara, to let them go and Barbara eventually acceded. Why wouldn't she? They lived in a safe neighborhood and the park would be teeming with visitors on such a gorgeous day. Besides, her oldest, Michella, was mature beyond her 12 years and could be trusted to watch over her younger siblings.

And so, the Welch sisters set off for Puget Park, a one-acre beauty spot bordering Commencement Bay. They arrived just after 11:30 and it was then that they realized they'd forgotten to bring the paper bag containing their packed lunch. "I'll ride back and fetch it," Michella told her sisters. "You guys stay here." She then departed, leaving them with a stern warning not to wander off. Angela and Nichole promised that they'd stay put.

However, about a half-hour after their big sister left, Angela and Nichole felt the call of nature. Since there was no public restroom in the park, they decided to cross the road and ask if they could use the facilities at one of the businesses there. They were confident that they'd be back before Michella, but they were wrong. When they returned, they found her Schwinn leaning up against a picnic table, the bag containing their lunch sitting on the table beside it. Of Michella, though, there was no sign.

At first, this did not particularly alarm the girls. They assumed that Michella had gone looking for them and would soon return. When she did, they could expect one of her 'big sister lectures.' But as the minutes ticked by and Michella did not appear, they began to worry. Eventually, they started looking for their sister, calling her name. When that failed to get a response, they went back to the hair salon where they'd earlier used the bathroom and asked if they could call their mom at work. Barbara Leonard listened with increasing alarm as Angela explained what had happened. She told her and Nichole to stay where they were until she got there. Then she hung up the phone and called the police.

By 3 p.m., a search of Puget Park and its surrounding area was underway by a small contingent of police. By six, search and rescue were called in, along with a K-9 team. It was just after 11:30 when one of the dogs found Michella Welch. The little girl was discovered in a ravine in a densely wooded part of the park. She had been throttled and badly beaten and her throat was slashed. The autopsy would reveal that she had been sexually assaulted.

In the aftermath of this terrible murder, a report surfaced of a man seen lurking in the shadows, watching the girls. That generated an identikit and a slew of leads. One of the most promising came from a man named Robert Washburn who said that he'd been jogging in nearby Point Defiance Park when he spotted a man who fit the description of the suspect. According to Washburn, the man was "acting suspiciously." This lead, unfortunately, led nowhere.

The community was up in arms. A little girl was dead, a child killer loose on the streets. What was the Tacoma Police Department going to do about it? In truth, Tacoma PD could not be faulted for its diligence. Detectives worked the case hard, drawing blanks at every turn. The best line of inquiry was the semen retrieved from the victim's body, but DNA profiling was still in its infancy back then, and CODIS was still three years in the future. The case was slipping away. Then, on August 4, 1986, another child was missing.

At 13, Jennifer Bastian was only slightly older than Michella Welch. A keen cyclist, Jenni was a member of a biking club and was looking forward to competing in an upcoming tour. That afternoon, she called her dad at work and asked if she could do a five-mile training loop of Point Defiance Park on her new bike. He told her that was fine, but that she should be home by 6:30.

Only Jenni wasn't home by 6:30, or by 7:30, or 8:30. The police were called and started a search of the park, bringing in the bloodhounds at 11:00 p.m. The dogs had helped find Michella Welch, but they were unsuccessful in this case. Jenni Bastian would be missing for three weeks before her body was discovered by a pair of joggers, buried under vegetation deep in the park. She had been sexually assaulted and strangled to death.

The method of murder was different, but the ages of the victims and the proximity of the crime scenes suggested a link. Investigators were convinced that a single perpetrator was responsible for both deaths. That made him a serial child killer, a terrifying prospect in a community with so many young families. As word of this latest atrocity spread, a siege mentality descended on the city of Tacoma. Home security was beefed up, children were kept off the streets, sales of firearms and ammunition spiked.

Meanwhile, the police identified a convicted child killer named David Fisher as their prime suspect and launched a concerted effort to track him down. Fisher, though, wasn't making it easy for them. He would remain at large for three years. When he was eventually arrested, DNA cleared him. That was in 1989. By then, the investigation was already in deep trouble. Soon, it would stall completely.

Step forward in time two decades to 2011, and we find the Tacoma Police Department establishing a Cold Case unit, under the leadership of Detective Gene Miller. Miller had been a patrol officer at the time of the Welch and Bastian murders. One of his investigators, Det. Lindsey Wade, had been just 11 years old back then, similar in age to the victims. She could well remember the pall of fear she'd lived under at the time. In part, it was what had inspired her to sign up for the police academy straight out of high school. Now, Wade would get a crack at the case that had haunted her for over two decades.

During that time, the prevailing theory was that a single perpetrator was responsible for the deaths of Michella Welch and Jenni Bastian. However, it had never been possible to test the hypothesis since no biological material had been retrieved from the Bastian crime scene. Now, as Det. Wade looked over the evidence again, she realized that the bathing suit Jenni had been wearing had never been tested. This was now submitted to the lab and a semen stain was detected, producing a viable DNA profile.

It was here that the case took an unexpected turn. The profile was different from the one found in the Welch case. The police had always believed that a monster had snuffed out two young lives in the summer of '86 in Tacoma. Turns out they were wrong. There was not one monster, but two.

Had either of these profiles found a match in CODIS at that time, then the police would at least have had something to show for their efforts. Frustratingly, there was no hit from the national database. Unperturbed, Det. Wade started working through the nearly 200 suspects that had been identified over the course of the two investigations. This was a mammoth task. Wade had to track down the men, ask them to submit to a test, and then send the samples to the lab for comparison and elimination. It was time-consuming and expensive. It is a testament to the resilience of the detective that she managed to process 160 of the 200 suspects before her retirement in 2018.

Lindsey Wade left the force believing that she'd failed. She was wrong. Just weeks into her retirement, she got a call from the detective who had taken over her cases. They had a match from the last batch of samples she'd submitted. The killer of Jenni Bastian had been identified. His name was Robert Washburn, the same Robert Washburn whose name had appeared as a witness in the Welch inquiry. He was the jogger who'd called the police to report that he'd seen a man matching the description of Michella's killer. Washburn ultimately entered a guilty plea to murder and received a 27-year prison term. It remains a mystery why he sought to insert himself into the Welch inquiry just months before he committed an atrocity of his own.

One of the two killers was in custody. The other, as yet, had not been caught, having evaded justice for over three decades. But the Tacoma police were not giving up. Encouraged by the Washburn result, cold case detectives gave approval for Parabon NanoLabs to upload DNA data from Michella Welch's killer to GEDmatch. This is a public, genetic genealogy database whose users voluntarily upload their DNA profiles, usually in the hope of tracing long-lost relatives. It has already been used by law enforcement to close several high-profile cold cases, most notably that of the Golden State Killer.

In this case, the results highlighted two brothers as potential suspects. The siblings were placed under police surveillance, with officers tracking them to retrieve any discarded object that might contain biological material – a soda can, a cigarette butt, a drinking straw. Here, it was a paper napkin, left behind at a fast-food restaurant, that would provide the breakthrough. The item was rushed to the lab where a profile was extracted. The comparison returned a match. Just like that, a decades-old mystery was resolved.

The suspect's name was Gary Charles Hartman, he was 66 years old and until recently had worked at Western State Hospital as a psychiatric nurse. Hartman had a clean criminal record. His neighbors described him as a "nice guy, kind, always smiling." He was married. He enjoyed restoring vintage cars. A Tacoma native, Hartman had lived his entire life in the city. He'd been living within a mile of Puget Park back in 1986, when 12-year-old Michella Welch was murdered. Aside from that atrocious crime, Gary Hartman had never gotten so much as a parking ticket in his life.

But now, Hartman stood accused of the ultimate evil. Arrested and brought before the courts in 2021, he initially entered a not guilty plea to murder. Later, after being convicted and sentenced to 26 years and six months in prison, he broke down and admitted his guilt. "I'm so sorry," he wept. "God knows I'm so sorry. That doesn't help. I'm just sorry." He will have plenty of time to contemplate his evil deed behind bars. More than likely, he will die there.

During the summer of 1986, two promising young lives were cut short in Tacoma, Washington. Michella Welch was 12 years old with blonde hair. She wore a pair of wire-framed glasses perched on her nose. Michella was a talented musician who excelled at the piano and violin. She was devoted to her younger sisters. Jennifer Bastian wore her blonde hair boyishly short and had strikingly blue eyes. She was an athletic 13-year-old who loved racing her bike and had already competed in several cycling tours. Who knows where that might have led, but for the intervention of a monster. Two innocent girls, two heartless killers, one black summer.

Bad Obsession

This was one of the most bizarre murders that Philadelphia PD had ever had to deal with, the seemingly motiveless killing of a Drexel University student. It happened on the night of November 30, 1984, when 20-year-old math major Deborah Wilson was burning the midnight oil, studying in the computer lab and running copies of course materials. Deborah was alone that night but that was no problem. The campus was patrolled by Wells Fargo security, with two guards on duty. The shift change was at midnight. At that time, the departing guard told his colleague that there was a female student working in the computer lab and asked him to walk her to her car once she was done. The incoming guard, David Dickson, said that he would.

Deborah Wilson could not have asked for a better protector. David Dickson was ex-military, and he held a black belt in karate. He knew how to handle himself. But Dickson would err in his duties this night. Deborah Wilson never made it to her car. Deborah would be found strangled to death in a stairway the next morning.

What was truly baffling about this crime was the apparent lack of motive. Deborah had not been raped and she had not been robbed. Her purse was on the ground beside her and had not been touched. The only thing the killer had taken was her shoes, believed to be a pair of white Reeboks. He'd also removed her socks and carried them away with him. Was this why the young woman had been killed? For her sneakers? As a motive, that simply didn't make sense.

The obvious place to start this investigation was by questioning the guards, especially David Dickson who had responsibility for the quadrant where the body was found. But Dickson had little to share with investigators. According to him, he'd passed by the computer lab at 1:30 a.m. and had heard the printer still running. Not wanting to disturb whoever was there, he had not entered. On his next pass, all was quiet, and the lights had been turned off. He'd assumed that the student had finished her work and left. He'd neither seen nor heard anything untoward.

It is uncertain how hard the investigators pressed Dickson, whether they believed his story or whether they considered him a person of interest. The case file suggests that they did not suspect him of involvement in Deborah Wilson's death. In any case, Dickson quit his job soon after and rejoined the Army. The case, meanwhile, went cold. It would remain so until 1992, when the Philadelphia authorities asked the Vidocq Society to take a look at it.

The Vidocq Society is a unique assemblage of retired law enforcement officials. It includes among its ranks former FBI profilers, homicide investigators, scientists, psychologists, prosecutors, and coroners, who contribute their time and expertise free of charge. The society meets regularly to consider cold cases presented to them by various jurisdictions. With such a wealth of experience, this is an invaluable resource, responsible for solving countless 'uncrackable' cases. In the Wilson murder inquiry, members quickly homed in on a detail that should have been obvious to the original investigators. The man they were looking for was a foot fetishist. That was why he'd taken Deborah Wilson's sneakers and not her purse.

With this key piece of information in hand, Philadelphia PD investigators went back to the case files to see what they might have missed. They immediately picked up on inconsistencies in the statement given by David Dickson. Dickson had stated that he'd heard the printer running when he passed by the computer lab at 1:30 a.m. However, this wasn't possible since university administrators had told detectives in a separate interview that the printers automatically shut down at 10:00 p.m. Somehow, the original investigative team had missed this discrepancy. Now, it brought laser focus on the former security guard.

And the more that detectives delved into David Dickson's background, the more they sat up and paid attention. Dickson's initial departure from the military had come under peculiar circumstances. Back in 1979, while Dickson was serving in Korea, the base was plagued by a bizarre crime wave. Several homes were broken into, with the burglar taking nothing but women's footwear. He seemed particularly interested in white sneakers. All other shoes were ignored. The military police launched an investigation and eventually identified the culprit, PFC David

Dickson. Hauled before a court-martial, Dickson was found guilty and drummed out of the military on a general discharge. The offenses were not considered serious enough to discharge him dishonorably. After his departure, Dickson was even allowed to join the Army Reserve, where he was promoted to sergeant.

But Dickson wasn't done yet with his shoe-stealing ways. While based as a reservist at the Philadelphia Naval Base, he went on another burglary spree. Soon, military wives were complaining to the authorities that their white sneakers were being pilfered. These complaints were not taken seriously. The base commander was convinced that they were a prank, perpetrated by women who had too much time on their hands while their husbands were away at sea. The matter went no further.

The next place that David Dickson's shoe obsession got him into trouble was in the corporate world. While employed as a maintenance man at SmithKline Beecham, he started obsessing over a fellow employee. First, he sent her a sexually explicit letter, anonymously penned, heavy on foot-related innuendo. Then he started calling her, whispering down the phone that he was going to rape her. Fortunately, he was caught before he could follow through on that threat. Dickson was fired from his job but faced no further action since his victim declined to file charges. A short time later, he was employed by Wells Fargo.

The Vidocq Society had advised the police to look for a killer with a foot fetish. Here was a man who clearly had a thing for women's feet, who had been alone in an empty building with the victim, who had lied in his original statement. No physical evidence connected him to the murder, but the circumstantial case was strong. In September 1993, the police moved in and placed Dickson under arrest.

A search of the suspect's house would provide a wealth of corroborating evidence. Dickson had a vast collection of what could best be described as "foot pornography." There were 77 videotapes in total. Some were quite innocent, showing girls in sneakers playing sports or just walking. Others were more hardcore, depicting sexual acts, toe-sucking, and other foot-related porn. One snippet showed a mannequin dressed in a pair of Keds. Then there was Dickson's shoe collection, over twenty pairs of white women's sneakers, contained within a steel trunk in his room. Each shoe was individually wrapped in plastic, like a collection of rare baseball cards. Unfortunately, Deborah Wilson's sneakers were not among them. It would have made the State's case had they been there.

Still, the D.A. was determined to bring the matter to trial, betting that the circumstantial evidence would be enough to convince a jury. The prosecution theory was that Dickson had spotted Deborah Wilson in the computer lab and been aroused by the white Reeboks she was wearing. He had decided that he wanted them and had attacked Deborah as she left the lab. A 'karate chop' had incapacitated the young woman. Dickson then dragged her into the stairwell and removed her shoes and socks. After that, there was no turning back. Dickson must have known that he'd be caught. His only way out was to kill his victim. He'd snuffed out Deborah's life with his hands on her throat.

Defense attorney Harry Seay was scathing in his rejection of the prosecution case. "There's no question he has a fetish," Seay told the court. "But if that fetish turns men into killers how come we don't have hundreds of homicides of girls with missing sneakers?" Even those on the prosecution team must have realized that he had a point. The jury was left with a far from straightforward decision.

Who can fathom the taking of a life for a pair of shoes? Certainly not the jurors at David Dickson's trial. They were hopelessly deadlocked, resulting in the judge declaring a mistrial.

Second time around, the prosecution had additional firepower. Like most criminals who think they are smarter than law enforcement, Dickson just could not help bragging about his misdeeds. He boasted to a fellow inmate about killing Deborah. That inmate turned snitch and informed the police. Jailhouse 'confessions' are hardly the most reliable foundation to build a case on but this one contained several telling details, including a description of the bruises on the victim's feet. Only the killer could have known these specifics. It would end up sinking the defense case.

David Dickson was found guilty of second-degree murder in 1997. He was sentenced to life in prison.

The Gambler

There's a reason that Las Vegas is known as Sin City. The 'Gambling Capital of the World' is a theme park for hedonists. Whatever your pleasure, whatever your vice, you'll find it here. All it takes is money. Marcus Bebb-Jones knew that as well as anyone.

Marcus was a UK national, raised by his grandmother in the West Midlands of England. Here, he grew to be a bright and articulate boy, with a head for figures and a sharp analytical mind. A job in manufacturing straight out of high school was considered a stop-gap before he went on to bigger and better things. But then the company folded and Marcus was out of work, eventually reduced to earning his living as a potato picker. That hadn't been in the plan. In the late 80s, he decided it was time for a change of scenery. Scraping together enough money for an airline ticket, he boarded a plane for the United States. He arrived as a tourist. It was always his intention to overstay his welcome.

Fast forward a few months and we find Marcus in Las Vegas. The city held an obvious attraction for him. He appreciated its brash, neon-lit charm and was a keen student of gambling. For now, though, he had to content himself with a backpackers' hostel and a series of minimum-wage jobs. It was at the hostel that he met a young Vietnamese woman named Sabrina.

It is uncertain what the pretty hotel management graduate saw in paunchy, prematurely balding Marcus. Nonetheless, there was a spark. The two started dating and were soon an item. They married in January 1993 and shortly thereafter moved to Grand Junction, Colorado. They'd picked up the lease on a run-down hotel here and figured they could turn it around. The happy picture was completed with the birth of their son, Daniel, in February 1994.

But it was here that things started to go wrong. The Melrose Hotel was proving more of a challenge than they had anticipated. The hotel was struggling financially and other problems were creeping into the relationship. Sabrina was a possessive woman and Marcus was the flirtatious type. Hotel staff witnessed frequent, blazing rows, usually over money or over Marcus's habit of hitting on female guests. By 1997, Sabrina was ready to throw in the towel. She told her husband that she wanted a divorce.

On the morning of September 15, 1997, Marcus Bebb-Jones loaded his wife and son into the family van and told hotel staff that they were taking a day trip to Dinosaur National Monument on the Colorado-Utah border. When they returned that night, however, one member of the family was conspicuously missing. According to Marcus, he and Sabrina had gotten into an argument, and she'd stormed off when they stopped at a shopping mall for a takeaway. He'd been unable to find her and suspected that she may have boarded a bus for Las Vegas, where she had family.

By the following morning, Marcus appeared to have regained his resolve to track down his wife. He informed his staff that he was driving to Las Vegas to look for her. He left soon after, with three-year-old Daniel strapped into the passenger seat. However, this was no rescue mission, no last-ditch attempt to save his failing marriage. Arriving in the city, Marcus checked into a suite at the Flamingo Hilton Hotel and hired himself a Ferrari. He then hit the town in a hedonistic 48-hour binge, during which he blew thousands of dollars on cocaine, hookers, and gambling, most of this financed on his wife's credit card. Then, as the money ran out and the card began to be declined, he skulked back to his room.

Marcus was at a different hotel now. Back at the Flamingo Hilton, staff had just found a hungry and dehydrated Daniel, wandering naked and crying through the halls. The toddler had been left unattended and unfed for two whole days at this point. Meanwhile, Marcus was in the room, scrawling a note on hotel stationery. 'Sabrina, I can't change who I am,' he wrote. 'I understand your anger, but know, as the years pass, that will diminish. This is the only way I can be without you or Daniel. Please don't hate me. Marcus.' The note completed, he placed the barrel of a .25 caliber handgun in his mouth and pulled the trigger.

Marcus Bebb-Jones did not succeed in this suicide attempt. The barrel shifted as he pulled the trigger and the bullet punched through his cheek rather than burying itself in his brain. He was found by hotel staff soon after and transported to a hospital and from there to a psychiatric ward. Here, he was visited by detectives, asking questions regarding the whereabouts of his wife. Sabrina's staff at the Melrose Hotel had reported her missing. Marcus repeated the story he'd told before, claiming that Sabrina had stormed off during an argument. The cops didn't believe him.

And they had good reason for their suspicions. An examination of Marcus's van turned up traces of blood, while an inspection of the undercarriage suggested that the vehicle had recently been driven off-road. Several purple, thistle-like blooms were caught in the chassis. The suicide attempt, too, seemed bogus. The police were convinced that Marcus had never intended to kill himself, that he'd staged the whole thing as part of some elaborate ploy, perhaps to cover up the murder of his wife. Still with nobody and zero evidence that a crime had been committed, there was little they could do. Bebb-Jones was free to go.

In the aftermath of his supposed suicide attempt, Marcus put the Melrose Hotel up for sale at a knock-down price. Half of the proceeds went to him, the balance into an escrow account in his wife's name. He then decamped for Las Vegas, where he'd spend the next two years living the shiftless life of a gambler. For a time, he cohabited with a female blackjack dealer. More commonly, he'd be seen with hired company on his arm. Bebb-Jones was moderately successful at the tables, but his lifestyle took a toll on his winnings. By 1999, he was broke. That same year, he returned to Britain.

Back on home soil, Marcus quickly offloaded Daniel on his parents, who would raise the boy. Then he rented a modest semi-detached home in the town of Kidderminster and resumed his career as a professional gambler. In Vegas, he'd been a small fish among sharks. Here in the UK, he was big-time. Days were spent playing poker online. By night, he'd usually be found at a Nottingham gambling den called Dusk Till Dawn. Bebb-Jones also entered various tournaments. In 2006, he reached the final of the £500,000 William Hill Grand Prix. A year later, he walked away with £90,000 at the Grosvenor Grand Prix Texas Hold 'Em event. The money paid for a comfortable lifestyle, including regular trips to Thailand. Marcus Bebb-Jones may have lost his wife and his business, but he'd come out of it alright.

What Marcus didn't know was that there was another game of chance underway, a game that was about to deal him the worst hand he'd ever drawn. In 2004, a cattle rancher was scouting a remote meadow in Garfield County, Colorado, when he came across a human skull. The police were called, and it was determined that the victim had died from a bullet wound to the head. Dental work would provide an identity. It was Sabrina Bebb-Jones. Interestingly, the meadow where the skull was found was dotted with clumps of purple thistle, the same plant that the police had found caught up in the undercarriage of Marcus's van.

Now followed a protracted investigation, lasting five years before the state of Colorado eventually had enough evidence to file murder charges. Application was then made to extradite Bebb-Jones to the U.S. Almost immediately, this hit a snag. The U.K. government would not grant the order if there was a chance that Bebb-Jones might face the death penalty. It was only when the U.S.

authorities agreed not to pursue a capital case, that the paperwork
was signed. In February of 2011, Marcus Bebb-Jones was jetting
his way back to the United States, not as a high roller this time or
even as a hopeful migrant. Now, he was a criminal defendant in a
murder case.

Initially, Bebb-Jones hung tough, sticking to his story, and refusing
to admit involvement in his wife's death. But as a poker player, he
must have known that he was holding a losing hand. The case
against him was solid and the penalty for conviction was high. He
wasn't going to bluff his way out of this one. Facing the prospect of
life in prison with no parole, Bebb-Jones struck a deal with
prosecutors and agreed to plead guilty to second-degree murder.
He still wouldn't admit to a pre-meditated act of violence though.
Despite evidence that Sabrina had been shot in the head, he
insisted that he had struck and killed her "in the heat of passion"
during an argument.

It is easy to understand Bebb-Jones's reticence to admit the truth.
To do so would be to confess to a decidedly callous act.
Investigators believe that he planned the murder to prevent his
wife from divorcing him, which would have been financially
ruinous. He'd lured Sabrina out into the wilderness on the
pretense of a family outing, then snuck up behind her and shot her
in the back of the head, presumably while she stood admiring the
scenery. We don't know where Daniel was at this time. Quite
possibly, the toddler witnessed his mother's murder.

Then, having committed this cowardly act, Bebb-Jones dragged
Sabrina into the undergrowth and pointed his van in the direction

of Vegas. He'd spend the next 48 hours getting high and partying with hookers, while his wife's body lay decaying in a field and being picked apart by scavengers.

Marcus Bebb-Jones was sentenced to life in prison and must serve at least 20 years before he is eligible for parole. The gambler had played his hand and lost. For the next two decades at least, his high-stakes games will be played for cigarettes and commissary credits.

American Nightmare

It was April 1975. The war in Vietnam was over. America was withdrawing its troops. On the streets of Saigon, panic reigned as the local population awaited the arrival of the North Vietnamese forces. Operation Frequent Wind was underway, evacuating those civilians lucky enough to have a ride out aboard an American chopper. On April 30, with People's Army of Vietnam tanks entering the city, the last Marines vacated the U.S. embassy building. For those left behind, the future looked dire.

And for some, the fall of the city represented an even greater fear. Particularly at risk were those who were seen to have collaborated with the Americans. Savang Phovixay, a Laotian national, had served as an adviser to the American forces and was thus a prime target for the new Communist regime. He was arrested, imprisoned, tortured. He would likely have died behind bars but for the efforts of his wife, Kham. She sold off every possession that the family had to raise enough money to bribe the guards at the prison. That was how Savang got out, but much danger still lay ahead. He and his family would make a daring escape aboard a makeshift raft. Eventually, they reached a refugee camp and secured passage to America.

Having paid such a high price for their freedom, Savang and Kham were determined to make the most of their new life. They would have plenty of help in that regard. During that era, it was quite common for churches to "adopt" incoming refugees, to help them settle, to smooth the difficult path of assimilation. In the case of the

Phovixay family, it was the First Baptist Church in Newnan, Georgia that took on the responsibility, finding them a house, helping them adapt to the culture and language, registering the children at local schools, even assisting the family with grocery shopping. The Phovixays repaid this kindness by working at the church. Savang did maintenance work. Kham helped out in the nursery.

Fast forward seven years and we find the family settled and thriving in Newnan. Savang and Kham are still having difficulty with the language, but the kids are doing well in school and have become quite 'Americanized.' The eldest, Vieng, has already graduated high school and is employed at Thriftown Foods, a grocery store in downtown Newnan. At 19, she has an American boyfriend named Ken Baker who lives at a mobile home park in nearby Moreland.

On the morning of October 10, 1987, Vieng Phovixay set off for work as usual, telling her parents that she'd be stopping off to visit Ken on her way in. Sometime later, she called her father, telling him that she had a flat on U.S. Hwy. 29, just south of I-85. Savang told her to wait there. He was on his way. Regrettably, Vieng did not abide by his instruction. When Savang arrived some minutes later, he found her Datsun pickup parked at the roadside with a flat tire. Of Vieng, there was no trace.

A missing person report was filed that day, with officers then dispatched to question Ken Baker. He confirmed that Vieng had visited him that morning. She'd left soon after, he said, but had returned to his trailer within ten minutes, driven by a burly, white man in a green 1975 Chevrolet El Camino with a white roof. Vieng had explained that she'd had a flat and that this stranger had stopped to help her. The man then drove off but later returned with a spare tire for Vieng's vehicle. She then left with him again, presumably to fix the car. That was the last time that Baker, or anyone else, had seen her.

The missing person case had now turned into a major investigation. While a search was underway, detectives got to work trying to identify the stranger who Vieng had driven off with. The man was described as late 30s to early 40s, heavyset, bearded, and wearing wire-framed glasses. At least two residents of the trailer park had seen the man and his vehicle. However, neither of them could pick him out of a photo array. What had looked like a strong lead, was slipping away. Meanwhile, the search to find Vieng Phoxivay was also faltering. Eventually, it would be abandoned altogether.

That was how things stood for the next two years. Then, in November 1989, a timberman was marking trees in a remote area of Harris County when he came across a human skull. He left the macabre artifact where he'd found it and completed his shift, only reporting it to the police that evening. The following morning, he led officers back to the site, where more skeletal remains were recovered, along with a white blouse, a knitted sweater, and strips of cloth tied into knots. From this evidence, officers deduced that the female victim had been tied to a tree with strips of her clothing, sexually assaulted, and then killed. They suspected that it may be Vieng Phoxivay but couldn't be sure. It would take more than two years of forensic work before the remains were positively identified. In October 1991, four years after her disappearance, Vieng was brought back to Newnan and buried at Oak Hill Cemetery.

The discovery of the remains gave fresh impetus to the case. Agents of the Georgia Bureau of Investigation (GBI) went over the evidence again, followed the leads, reinterviewed witnesses. A photo array was again presented to witnesses but again came up empty. None of them could make a positive identification. For a second time, the investigation went cold.

For one officer, though, the case never really went away. In March of 2005, GBI agent Gary Rothwell met up with investigator Clay Bryant of the Georgia State Attorney's office. The two started talking about the Phovixay case with Rothwell admitting that the case had always bugged him and that he believed it could be solved. By the end of that conversation, Bryant had agreed to take another look at the evidence, beginning with the eyewitness sightings of the man in the El Camino.

Three witnesses had seen this man on the day that Vieng disappeared – Ken Baker, his neighbor, Lucretia Boynton, and another resident of the park, Johnny Wentz. Twice before they had failed to pick out the suspect, but this time would be different. With the photographs spread out in from of them, each unerringly pointed to the same man – Charles Travis Manley.

There was a good reason why Manley was in the lineup. Not only was he a good physical match for the description of the suspect, but he was also a three-time convicted sex offender. His first offense was the knife-point rape of a 15-year-old. The second, involved spousal rape. Manley had placed a gun to his wife's head and forced her to have sex. In the third incident, Manley abducted a teenage couple, forced the boy into the trunk of his car, then assaulted the girl in the back seat.

Manley had served time for each of the crimes, but he was free when Vieng disappeared, free and driving a green 1975 El Camino, just like the one the young woman had been driven away in. Suspiciously, he'd had the vehicle sprayed a different color while the search for Vieng was underway. Then, after Vieng's remains were discovered in 1989, he'd sold the car to an out-of-state buyer. That looked suspicious. Charles Manley had some questions to answer.

And his answers to those questions came down to one thing. The eyewitnesses were mistaken. They may have put him at the scene and placed the victim in his car, but he was innocent. Manley was charged anyway, and brought to trial in 2007, entering a not guilty plea. Here, his defense offered up an alternate suspect, Vieng's boyfriend, Ken Baker.

According to this theory, the relationship was volatile, punctuated by frequent fights and breakups. Another of those altercations occurred on October 10, 1987, and this time Ken had snapped and killed Vieng. Presumably, he'd then transported his girlfriend's body to a remote area and tied her to a tree for some obscure reason. Presumably, he'd also driven her car to Highway 29, punctured the tire, and then called Vieng's father and successfully imitated her in a language he didn't speak. He'd also roped in two of his neighbors to frame Charles Manley, a man none of them had ever met.

This version of events doesn't make sense and it wasn't meant to. Its sole purpose was to raise doubt in the minds of the jurors, and it nearly worked. When the jury returned for the first time, the foreman announced that they were deadlocked. The judge then sent them back for further deliberation. This time, the verdict was "guilty." Charles Manley slumped back in his seat and started crying when it was announced. He was still protesting his innocence when the judge handed down a life sentence.

Witness impact statements are usually the most poignant part of a murder trial and in this case, it was doubly so. Here was a family who had escaped the ravages of war, who had risked life and limb to make it to safety, only for their American dream to turn into an American nightmare. "We came to the United States 27 years ago looking for a life of hope and a new beginning," Vieng's sister, Amphay, said in a statement. "Our hope for a new and happier life was shattered when our older sister, Vieng, was brutally taken away from us. This tragedy has affected us in ways that words can't describe."

Charles Travis Manley would serve less than eight years of his life sentence. He died in prison of natural causes on January 23, 2015.

After the Fire

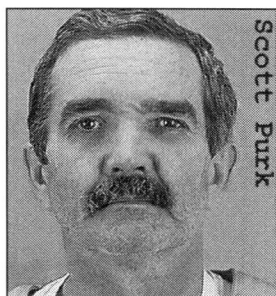

Scott Purk

On the morning of March 18, 1985, a desperate call came into the emergency services in Stow, Ohio. The man on the line identified himself as Scott Purk and said that his wife had tried to kill herself. First responders were immediately dispatched to the address and found 24-year-old Margaret "Meg" Purk, lying at the base of the stairs, a rope around her neck. Meg was heavily pregnant, and she had no pulse, no heartbeat. The situation seemed hopeless, but paramedics got to work immediately, trying to save the young woman and her unborn child. Miraculously, they managed to get her breathing again and continued their lifesaving efforts on the way to the hospital. There, ER doctors took over and declared themselves optimistic that Meg would make it. It seemed that a double tragedy had been averted.

But that initial optimism would prove unfounded. Within hours, Meg Purk's condition worsened, and she slipped away, despite the desperate efforts of medical staff. She and her child were gone, and the circumstances of their deaths demanded answers. The man of whom those answers were required, was her husband Scott.

For someone who had just lost his wife and child to a terrible tragedy, Scott Purk was remarkably calm as he sat down with detectives. He said that Meg had been excited about her pregnancy early on and had been looking forward to becoming a mom. However, as the date got closer, her mood darkened. By her final trimester, she had become dejected, melancholy, weepy-eyed. This condition is called prenatal depression and is quite common in expectant mothers, affecting approximately one in seven. Scott did what he could to console his wife, to assure her that all would be well. He never expected that she'd "do something crazy."

On the morning of Meg's death, according to Scott, he was soaking in the bath when he saw her walk past, in the direction of the stairs. Her demeanor concerned him and so he got out of the water, toweled himself off, and went to check on her. That was when he saw her hanging from the second-floor railing. He immediately tried to get her down from there but the knot she'd tied to the banister was too tight and he couldn't loosen it. He ran to the kitchen to fetch a steak knife, which he used to hack through the rope. All the while, Meg was still hanging there, the life slowly being choked out of her. By the time he got her down, she appeared lifeless. He'd immediately run to the phone and called 911.

To investigators, Scott Purk's story sounded suspicious. In their experience, suicides seldom commit their desperate acts with someone nearby. Those who are serious about ending their lives usually wait until they are alone, with no one able to intervene. A detective asked if Meg had left a suicide note. Scott said that she had, and handed over a poem she'd written, expressing suicidal thoughts. However, during a search of the Purk residence, officers found something that directly contradicted this. It was a letter that Meg had penned to her grandmother just weeks earlier. In it, she was decidedly upbeat, positively gushing over the prospect of becoming a mom. How had she gone from that to taking her own life in such a short time?

These were questions that needed answers and the Stow Police Department got some of them when they spoke to Meg's family. Scott Purk was not well-liked by his in-laws. They said that he was a habitual liar and that he'd been "nothing but trouble" for Meg during their three-year marriage. As for the supposed "suicide note," Meg's family said that it was something she'd written years earlier. They admitted that she'd suffered from depression in the past but insisted that she had been well for years now. They also said that she'd been looking forward to the birth of her baby, which had been due within days of her death.

All of this painted Scott Purk in a bad light. But did it prove that he was lying? Did it flag his wife's death as anything other than the tragedy he claimed it to be? The simple answer was that it did not. The police might have had their suspicions about Purk but they had not a shred of evidence against him. Once the medical examiner ruled Margaret Purk's death as a suicide, the case was closed.

Shortly after Margaret Purk was laid to rest, the area around the Purk residence began to be plagued by a series of burglaries. These would continue for months before police eventually arrested the perpetrator. It was Scott Purk. Hauled before the courts, Purk offered a bizarre defense. He claimed that the break-ins were his way of dealing with his wife's death. The jury wasn't buying it and found him guilty as charged. He was sentenced to six years in prison.

Fast forward now to March of 2009. Scott Purk has long since served his time and is back in Stow, Ohio. He has remarried and has two children. For the most part, he is keeping a low profile. But drama and Scott Purk had never been far removed from each other. One night in March, his house caught fire and burned to the ground. Fortunately, Scott and his wife and kids escaped unhurt.

This was no accidental blaze. While examining the scene, detectives found clear signs of arson. Who had started the fire? The obvious suspect was the man of the house, but Purk denied this. He claimed that he'd been awakened by an explosion and had smelled smoke. He'd then got his family out of the house before calling 911. Purk had his own ideas as to who might be responsible. He handed detectives a list of license numbers which he claimed were from suspicious cars he'd seen in the neighborhood on the night of the fire.

And then, Scott Purk made an odd comment. He brought up the subject of his dead wife, now 24 years in the grave. He'd been suspected there too, he said, and had turned out to be innocent. Perhaps he thought that this would allay suspicion in the arson case. If anything, it had the opposite effect. Investigators were convinced that he was guilty of arson. They were also beginning to wonder if there was more to his wife's death than they knew.

Scott Purk does not appear to have been the brightest of criminals. Delving into the fire at his house, detectives soon learned that Purk was in debt to the tune of hundreds of thousands of dollars. He was also heavily insured and had recently shot a video documenting all the valuables in his house. These valuables had not escaped the blaze but, by some miracle, the video had. It all gave Purk a strong motive for setting the fire.

For now, the police lacked sufficient evidence to charge Purk with arson. But the comment he'd made about his dead wife had aroused the suspicions of detectives and so they decided to take a look at the case. What they found was stunning. Meg Purk had been discovered with a rope around her neck and the suggestion was that she'd used this rope to hang herself. But a rope leaves a particular bruising pattern and the bruises that were evident in the autopsy photos did not match this. They were too broad, too smooth, the kind of bruises that suggest strangulation with a belt.

Detectives also learned that Purk had moved in with another woman shortly after Meg died. Had he been having an affair? Was this a motive for murder? To find out, investigators tracked down the woman and questioned her. Her description of Scott was far from complimentary. She called him "crazy, horrible, just the craziest person I've ever met in my life." Then she dropped a bombshell. Purk had boasted to her that he'd killed his wife and gotten away with it.

This was a stunning allegation but one that would require corroborating evidence. The police were still contemplating how to do this when there was a second devastating fire in Stow. Again, the family escaped with their lives but lost all their possessions. In fact, the fire was so similar to the one at the Purk residence that the police immediately suspected a copycat. Their theory was that Scott had torched this second house to create the impression that there was a serial arsonist at work and thus throw the authorities off his scent. If that was his plan, it didn't work. When detectives visited Purk at his new apartment they found a gas canister and a pair of soot-covered work boots. Purk was arrested and charged with two counts of arson.

With Purk now in custody and awaiting trial for arson, the police turned their attention once again to the suspicious death of his former wife. The autopsy photos suggested that mistakes had been made during the original investigation. However, they were not evidence of murder. To settle the argument once and for all, there would have to be a new autopsy. On September 21, 2011, Meg Purk's long rest was disturbed as her body was brought to the surface.

Given that she had been dead for 26 years, Meg's remains were remarkably well preserved. This was good news for investigators, bad news for her former husband, Scott. It was relatively easy to determine that the marks around Meg's neck had not been made by a rope but by something with a smooth surface, probably a belt. Where the medical examiner did find rope burns was on the torso, just under the breasts. He surmised that a rope had been looped around the woman and used to drag her across the floor. Most probably, this was done to maneuver the body into a position that would support Purk's suicide story. It added yet another appalling component to this heartbreaking story.

Back in 1985, Meg Purk's death had been ruled a suicide. Now, the cause of death was altered to reflect homicide by strangulation. Given the circumstances of the case, there was only one suspect. Scott Purk was arrested and charged with first-degree murder.

By the time that Purk was brought to trial for murder in November 2015, he was already a convicted felon. Eighteen months earlier, he'd entered a guilty plea to two counts of aggravated arson and had been sentenced to 28 years in prison. Still, Purk wasn't about to admit to murder. He seemed confident of an acquittal, almost smug as he sat at the defense table and heard the evidence against him.

The prosecution case was simple. Purk claimed that his wife hung herself with a rope; the medical evidence proved that she had been strangled with a belt. Purk had lied about this and was the only other person in the house when Meg died. He had motive and opportunity. Therefore, he was the killer.

This was how the prosecutor argued and how the jury ruled. After a trial lasting six days, Scott Purk was found guilty as charged. He was sentenced to life in prison and must serve at least 15 years before he can apply for parole. Given that this sentence runs consecutive to his arson conviction, he will be in prison for a very long time. That is no more than this callous killer deserves. As one police officer remarked after the trial, "It takes a special type of coward to murder your pregnant wife and make everybody believe it was suicide."

Have Death, Will Travel

Bill Marquardt

It started with a request for a welfare check, called into a 911 line in Sumter County, Florida on March 15, 2000. A family member had been unable to contact 72-year-old Margarita Ruiz, and her daughter, 42-year-old Esperanza Wells. He asked if a cruiser could be sent to an address in Tarrytown, to check on them. He mentioned also that there were two infants in the household, Esperanza's children, aged one and three.

Officers were duly dispatched to the residence, a neat cottage somewhat isolated from its neighbors. They arrived to find something that had them immediately reaching for their weapons. The screen on the back door had been forced, with the latch hanging loose from its bracket. The officers entered with guns drawn. In the kitchen, they found even more cause for alarm. There was blood on the floor, blood sprayed across the walls and cabinetry. A bullet hole was punched into the door of the refrigerator. Calling out and getting no response, the officers proceeded carefully into the residence. A trail of blood was clearly visible in the hallway. Following it brought them to the master bedroom. That was where they found Margarita and Esperanza.

The older woman had been shot twice in the back and once in the chest. She had also been stabbed three times in the throat. Esperanza had been executed by a bullet to the head. The killer had then taken his knife to her, plunging it repeatedly into her neck. Sprays and spatters of blood spoke of a desperate struggle, of two women who had died in terror and pain. The only small mercy was that the children were not harmed. They were found hiding under the dining table, traumatized but otherwise unhurt.

So, who had perpetrated this atrocity, and why? That was a question that perplexed the police. The murders appeared entirely without motive. The killer, it seemed, had chosen the house at random, forced his way in, and slaughtered the occupants. Nothing had been taken from the property and the women had not been sexually molested. The motive for the murders seemed to be nothing but pure bloodlust. That greatly concerned investigators. A person of this mindset was very likely to kill again.

We now shift our focus to the other end of the country, to Chippewa Falls, Wisconsin, and to a crime that was committed two days prior to the double homicide in Tarrytown. On March 13, 2000, Alfred Marquardt returned home to find his wife, Mary Jane, missing. Alfred conducted a search and eventually found her lying on the cold concrete floor of the garage, surrounded by a pool of blood. Mary Jane had met a similar fate as Esperanza Wells and Margarita Ruiz. She had been shot and stabbed to death. In this case, though, there was a clear and obvious suspect, the dead woman's son, Bill.

Bill Marquardt was a young man with serious issues. This was an individual who was obsessed with violence, fascinated by death. He enjoyed killing animals and dissecting their corpses. He also had a small arsenal of weapons. Questioned about his whereabouts at the time of the murder, Bill said that he'd been in Florida. The police verified that he had made the trip but that he'd departed Wisconsin after his mother's murder. His alibi was invalid. Investigators then obtained a search warrant for his cabin in Eau Claire County. Here, among the decomposing corpses of several animals, they found a 9mm pistol and several boxes of ammunition.

Ballistics would show that this was the gun that had killed Mary Jane Marquardt. Additionally, detectives recovered a blood-encrusted pocketknife. DNA tests proved that some of that blood was from the murder victim. There were also two unidentified profiles. The police didn't know who those were from. All that the lab could tell them was that these two individuals were related.

On the face of it, this looked like the clearest of clear-cut cases. Bill Marquardt had been found with the murder weapon in his possession. His mother's blood was on a knife he owned. The Wisconsin Crime Lab had even recovered traces of Mary Jane's blood from his shoes. There should have been no question as to who was responsible.

But who knows how a jury will lean? At Marquardt's 2006 trial, the defense spun a fanciful tale of a drug-dealing father and son team who had it in for Bill and had killed his mother to frame him. Bill Marquardt was an upstanding young man, his lawyer assured the court. He'd loved his mother and would never have harmed her. Her death had caused him considerable grief. Now, that grief was being exacerbated by a police department that had been tardy in its work, focusing only on the suspect closest at hand and failing to dig deeper.

This was a classic defense tactic, aimed not at proving innocence but at creating reasonable doubt. In this case, the story was delivered with enough conviction to sway the jurors. They voted for acquittal.

The decision left everyone stunned, not least Chippewa County District Attorney Jon Theisen. Theisen had spent a sizable chunk of the last six years readying the case for trial. He'd been meticulous in his preparation. Seldom had he been more confident of a favorable outcome. Now, all of his work was undone. Worse still, the law of double jeopardy applied. Bill Marquardt could go on national television to admit that he'd killed his mother, and they couldn't touch him.

Fortunately, Jon Theisen was a sore loser. He wasn't going to take this lying down. Instead, he went back to the case file. The lab had lifted two unidentified DNA profiles from the dried blood on Marquardt's pocketknife. What if that blood was from another crime scene? What if there were victims besides Mary Jane? What if Bill Marquardt had done this more than once?

The problem for Theisen was that this possibility had already been explored back in 2000. Investigators had delved into every recent homicide in the state, looking for one that might match. They'd found nothing. Undeterred, Theisen sent out a statewide alert, asking law agencies to inform him of unsolved murders, circa early 2000, that might fit the profile of the Marquardt killing. All he got back was a deafening silence.

But still, Theisen wasn't ready to quit. He now recalled that Bill Marquardt had departed for Florida around the time of his mother's murder, and had even tried to use that trip as an alibi. Now Theisen reached out to the authorities there and soon had a response. There was a cold case in Sumter County, the unsolved murders of Margarita Ruiz and Esperanza Wells.

From here, it was just a case of matching up the evidence. The blood from Bill Marquardt's pocketknife was tested against the Florida victims. A match. Marquardt's 9mm was sent for ballistic tests. It matched the bullets retrieved from the two women. In addition, Marquardt's DNA was found at the scene. After six years, the Tarrytown murders were solved. And all because one disgruntled D.A. refused to take a loss.

Bill Marquardt's extradition to Florida would be a protracted process since Bill had since been convicted on animal cruelty charges and confined to a psychiatric facility after being diagnosed with paranoid schizophrenia. The paperwork was completed in 2011, and Marquardt was then transported to Florida to stand trial. He appeared before the courts in October of that year, offering a familiar defense. According to Bill, he'd been framed for the murders. The real culprits were a drug-dealing father and son duo from Wisconsin, the same men he'd accused of murdering his mother.

But what had worked so well for Marquardt before a Wisconsin jury, did not fly in Florida. He was found guilty on two counts of first-degree murder. Then came the sentencing phase, where Marquardt asked to be sentenced to death. The judge was happy to oblige him.

Bill Marquardt is currently incarcerated at the Union Correctional Institution in Raiford, Florida, where he awaits execution. His sentence was affirmed by the Florida Supreme Court in 2015.

Desperado

Lonnie Wiseman

1994 was a bad year for the city of Richmond, Virginia, its bloodiest in over a century. Nearly 160 homicides were recorded that year, the largest number of violent deaths since the Civil War. In among that carnage, the murder of 50-year-old Henry Weatherford was merely a statistic.

Weatherford was the proprietor of Honeybrook Antiques, a business he owned in partnership with a man named George Newby. It was Newby who found his bullet-riddled body on June 13, 1994, lying on a couch in the living room of his home, in the 5700 block of Crenshaw Road in Henrico County. The antiques dealer had been shot several times and the motive seemed obvious. Both his wallet and car were missing.

This was a murder that the Henrico County police had very little chance of solving. The Weatherford residence was remote, neighbors too far away to have seen or heard anything suspicious. The only clue to emerge was that Weatherford had recently been keeping company with a clean-cut young man, who he'd met on a recent antique hunting road trip to Georgia and Florida. No one knew this man's name or could even provide a detailed description of him. All that they could say was that he was a small, slightly built individual with sandy hair and that he was perhaps mid-20s. Henry had been keeping his new friend under wraps.

But what police did have was a description of the dead man's car, a late-model Oldsmobile. A BOLO alert was issued on the vehicle, but it would be a month before it was found, abandoned in a Wal-Mart parking lot in St. Louis. The car had been wiped clean of prints but there were some cigarette butts in the ashtray, which the police booked into evidence. Whoever had taken the vehicle, likely the man who'd shot Henry Weatherford, was long gone by then. Already, he had a month's start on the police. It was a gap they'd never close.

In the aftermath of Henry Weatherford's death, his partner, George Newby, sold off all the shop's inventory and shut down the business. Meanwhile, Henrico County investigators believed that they'd caught a break in the case. Between May and November 1994, a serial killer embarked on a bloody rampage through Maryland, Virginia, and Florida. Gary Ray Bowles had a well-worked routine. He'd befriend gay men, move into their homes, then kill them and rob them of their valuables. This fit the M.O. of the Weatherford murder almost exactly, leading detectives to speculate that Henry Weatherford might have fallen victim to the roving psychopath. However, Bowles, the killer of six men, denied this. He swore that Henry Weatherford wasn't one of his victims. With nothing to connect him to the crime, investigators had to take his word for it.

Then, in March of 1995, there was another twist. Weatherford's former partner was arrested for rape. George Newby had accepted a ride from a waitress in Chester, then forced himself on the woman, raping and sodomizing her. Arrested soon after, Newby would draw a heavy sentence, 85 years behind bars.

The severity of the sentence came as a shock to the former antiques trader, who had insisted throughout the trial that he was innocent and that the sex was consensual. But while Newby wasn't prepared to admit to rape, he was prepared to admit to another crime. Shortly after he started his sentence, he contacted Henrico County investigators and said that he had information that would clear up an unsolved homicide.

The murder that Newby was referencing was that of his former friend and business partner, Henry Weatherford. Newby was ready to take the rap, confessing that it was he who'd shot George. However, the confession was far from solid. There were several glaring errors and omissions. For example, Newby couldn't say where he'd gotten the murder weapon and what he'd done with it after the shooting. He also could not explain how Weatherford's Olds had ended up in St. Louis, 800 miles away.

As the questions became more probing, it became clear to the detectives that Newby was lying. Eventually, he cracked and admitted that he'd made the whole thing up. He'd wanted another day in court, he said, so that he could draw attention to his 'unjust' rape conviction. All he'd succeeded in doing was to waste valuable police time. At this point, the Weatherford investigation was dead in the water.

But the Henrico authorities had not yet given up on solving the case. In February of 1999, they posted information on the murder, along with four other cold cases, on their website, hoping that someone would come forward. When no one did, they turned to the forensic evidence. The cigarette butts found in the ashtray of Henry Weatherford's car were sent to the lab, where a DNA profile was extracted. Unfortunately, that profile did not find a match in any law enforcement database. The police would have to bide their time, hoping that their man slipped up and that his DNA ended up in CODIS.

What the police didn't know was that the man they sought was already in custody. His name was Lonnie Ray Wiseman, and he was a habitual criminal, at odds with society from the time he could walk. Lonnie Ray was a man born in the wrong era, a man whose inclinations would have been better suited to the Wild West. He'd have fit right into the James/Younger Gang or with Billy the Kid and the Regulators. In the words of one of the cops who pursued him, Lonnie Ray was a desperado. He was also a good physical match for the man seen in Henry Weatherford's company around the time he was killed. Right after that murder, Wiseman moved on from Richmond and hit the road.

In the weeks that followed, Lonnie Ray Wiseman would unleash a one-man crime wave across the Midwest, showing up in Kentucky, Indiana, and Ohio, carrying out a slew of holdups in each. Then, after being captured, tried, and sentenced to jail time in Idaho, he staged a daring escape from prison and did it all again.

Between August and December 1995, Wiseman and his fellow escapee, Tommy Martin, embarked on a new robbery spree, pulling off eight holdups of convenience stores and gas stations from New Mexico to Arkansas. The fugitives were eventually tracked down by Arkansas state troopers but fled in a stolen vehicle and engaged the officers in a high-speed chase. Wiseman was caught after their car spun out of control and left the road. Martin fled on foot but was arrested two weeks later in Abilene, Texas. For both men, it was a quick trip back to prison.

And there Lonnie Wiseman would remain until 2014, when his DNA was finally matched to evidence from the Weatherford case. Wiseman had by now done his time in Idaho and was incarcerated in Iowa for another crime. He was working in the woodworking shop and had attained a level of some artistry in crafting fine furniture. Finally, Lonnie had found a vocation he enjoyed that didn't involve criminality. He considered it a major inconvenience to be sent back to Virginia to stand trial for murder.

Wiseman did not admit to killing Henry Weatherford. In fact, he outright denied it. According to him, he did not know the man and had never met him. His only crime was taking Weatherford's Oldsmobile after he'd found it in a parking lot with the keys dangling invitingly from the ignition. That was how his DNA ended up on the cigarettes found in the ashtray. Yes, he'd used the car in a series of holdups. No, he hadn't murdered its owner.

This was Lonnie Wiseman's stance on the matter. However, he offered none of these arguments at trial, instead entering a plea of no contest and accepting a sentence of 23 years behind bars. It made no difference to him. With several states standing in line to lock him up once he finishes his time in Iowa, he knows that he will never be free. It is unlikely that he'll ever see the inside of a Virginia prison cell. Too many jurisdictions have a claim on him first. This desperado's days of raising hell are over.

Storm Warning

Rita Bado was making a fresh start. After a recent divorce, the 45-year-old had decided to leave her hometown of Torrington, Connecticut to move to Palm Beach County, Florida, where her brother lived. Joining her on this adventure would be her 20-year-old daughter, Lisa. The pair arrived in the Sunshine State in August of 1991. There, Rita got a job at Wal-Mart, while Lisa enrolled at the Florida Culinary Institute and found work at a seafood restaurant in Palm Beach. After living with relatives for a couple of months, mother and daughter moved into an apartment in the Runaway Bay complex in Lantana. With a place of their own, family in close proximity, and jobs they both liked, the move could not have gone any better.

But then came the morning of August 22, when Rita's brother, Thomas Tebecio, got a call from her supervisor, concerned that Rita hadn't shown up for work and hadn't called in. Rita also wasn't answering her phone. The supervisor wondered if Thomas had heard from her. Thomas said that he hadn't, but that he'd drive to Rita's apartment to check on her. He arrived to a locked door and got no response when he knocked. Then he peered through a window and noticed disarranged furniture in the living room. His next move was to find a phone and call 911.

Palm Beach officers were soon on the scene. After forcing the door, they cautioned Thomas and his wife Karen to remain in the hallway. That was a good thing. What lay inside was not for the faint of heart. Rita and her daughter were found trussed up in a bedroom. Both women had been executed by a bullet to the head but that told only part of the story. Whoever had done this was a psychopath and a sadist. He'd taken his time here, smoking four cigarettes while he tortured and abused the women.

Lisa Bado, in particular, had been made to suffer. Her body was covered in cuts and bruises. She had also been raped. Judging by the scene, detectives speculated that Rita had been made to watch her daughter being abused. She'd then been shot, with Lisa forced to watch before her own life was taken. Then, having molested and murdered the mother and daughter, the killer ransacked their home, loaded up their television set, and drove away in Rita's Honda CRX. The vehicle was later found abandoned in the parking lot of a Sam's Wholesale Club in Lantana. Unfortunately, it yielded no clues.

But detectives were able to retrieve valuable evidence from the scene itself. The killer had been smart enough to wipe down any surfaces he'd touched but dumb enough to leave behind four cigarette butts. These were bagged in the hope that they would yield a DNA profile. Crime scene technicians also found several hairs that were not from either of the victims. These, too, were bagged as evidence.

Before the investigation could gain any momentum, though, the police had a new crisis to deal with, bigger even than a brutal double homicide. Hurricane Andrew was bearing down on the coast of Florida. The storm, which would be classified as a Category 5, made landfall on August 24, just two days after the murders. It resulted in a mass evacuation of the area, with every available law officer seconded to the effort. All ongoing investigations were suspended.

Not that investigative work would have been possible amid such a calamity. Then, once the storm passed, there was the cleanup. By the time detectives were able to get back to work on the case, valuable time had been lost. They feared that the killer might have used the chaos to flee the state. That would turn out to be an accurate assessment.

This was an investigation that would lean heavily on the physical evidence. DNA profiling was still a fairly new technology in the early 90s, but it was advanced enough to extract a profile from the cigarette butts left at the scene. The problem was that there was nothing to compare it to. CODIS was still several years in the future. The mandatory collection of DNA samples from felons and arrestees was still a controversial topic. Indeed, it remains so to this day. It all meant that the DNA profile was of little use until the police had a suspect in custody. Right now, they had no one. They did, however, test their profile against 29 men in Rita and Lisa

Bado's circle – family members, friends, Lisa's classmates, even her tennis coach.

But this was a mere formality. The police never expected a match, and they didn't get one. Right from the start, investigators were convinced that this was a random act of violence, committed by some opportunistic psychopath. Given his fixation on Lisa, it was likely that he'd spotted her somewhere and followed her home. Since the door of the apartment hadn't been forced, detectives believed that he'd either bluffed his way in or that had entered through a door left carelessly unlocked.

Either way, this was a stranger killing, the hardest kind to solve. Investigators would consider nearly 1,000 suspects over the course of their inquiries, many of them convicted sex offenders living in the area. They came up empty at every turn. It seemed this was a case destined to wear the unwanted tag of "unsolved."

But then came the Combined DNA Index System, CODIS to the law enforcement officers who have come to rely so heavily on it. Initially piloted by the FBI in 1990, its use was authorized by the DNA Identification Act of 1994. Four years later, it was made available to law agencies in all 50 states. In 2001, the Palm Beach County Sheriff's Department submitted its profile from the Bado murders...and got a hit. The man that they'd been hunting for the past ten years was a habitual criminal named James Anthony Frederick.

James Frederick was not the kind of person you'd want to encounter in a dark alley, or even on a busy city street for that matter. Everyone who knew him, even his own brother, described him as a violent, brutal person. Frederick had spent most of his adult life building up a rap sheet that read like a summary of the penal code. There were arrests and convictions for auto theft, narcotics, resisting arrest, burglary, assault, attempted murder. At the time that his name first came up in connection with the Bado murders, he was serving a life term in Wisconsin for armed robbery.

That, of course, made him easy to find. However, Palm Beach investigators were in no hurry to make their move. After waiting ten years to close their case, they wanted to do this right. First, they needed to put Frederick in the vicinity of the crime scene at the time of the murders. That turned out to be easy. He'd been released from custody just two days earlier, having been arrested for assaulting a police officer.

Next, the police wanted a fallback position for their DNA evidence. Frederick could easily claim that he'd been a friend of Lisa Bado's and had smoked the cigarettes while visiting her, leaving behind the butts they'd found. The hairs, retrieved from a bedsheet, would negate that argument. These were sent to the lab for extraction and comparison of a DNA profile. The chances that it had come from anyone other than James Frederick were estimated at a quadrillion to one. It was time for Mr. Frederick to answer some questions.

Initially, Frederick denied having anything to do with the murders. Then investigators revealed that they had found his DNA at the scene, and Frederick simply shrugged. "I guess I'm going to Florida," he said. He would arrive there in 2005, facing a probable death sentence if convicted. Few would argue that he wouldn't have deserved it. But James Frederick valued his own life much more highly than he valued the lives of others. Desperate to avoid the needle, he agreed a deal with prosecutors, entering a guilty plea to two counts of first-degree murder and receiving two life terms with no possibility of parole.

James Anthony Frederick is currently an inmate at DOC Waupun Correctional Institution in Wisconsin, with a projected release date of 2099. In the unlikely event that he is paroled from that term, he will be sent to a prison in Florida, to see out the rest of his days.

Death Comes Calling

In 1976, the year that she graduated high school, Tana Woolley entered the Miss Rosamond beauty pageant and walked away with the crown. No one was really surprised that she won. Tana was a natural, not just beautiful but outgoing, wholesome, radiant. She was also a bright girl, who got a job as a secretary at NASA right out of school. At the same time, she started attending Antelope Valley College, working towards her degree. She hoped one day to work with handicapped children.

The Woolleys were a close-knit family. Tana was close to her parents and adored her three younger siblings. However, there comes a time when children strike out on their own and for Tana, that time arrived in October 1978. She'd found herself a neat apartment on Poplar Street in Rosamond and was looking forward to moving in and decorating the place to her taste. The lease was signed, and the security deposit paid. Tana was taking her first steps into the adult world.

However, just two weeks into her new adventure and Tana was
beginning to have second thoughts about living alone. To friends,
she confided that she was feeling uneasy in the apartment, feeling
as though someone was watching her. Those friends told her that
it was only natural to feel that way. After all, she'd gone from a
boisterous household where there was always someone around, to
living solo. Tana conceded that they were probably right. Still, she
developed some decidedly paranoid habits. She would not answer
a knock at her door without first peering out through the window
to see who was there. She also moved out of her bedroom and set
up a bed in the living room, which didn't have an outward-facing
window.

Also living at the Poplar Street apartment block at this time was a
man named Larry Hazlett Jr. Hazlett was Tana's neighbor. The rear
window of his unit looked out on her front door, just ten feet away.
Tana hadn't met him yet, but Larry had a reputation in the
building. He was the local creep, the guy who stalked the corridors,
leering at female residents and sometimes making improper
suggestions. When these crude advances were rejected, Larry
would usually get angry and cry racism. Threats were issued on
occasion and one woman accused him of stalking her. All of them
quickly learned to avoid him.

On the night of Tuesday, October 24, Tana Woolley spent a
pleasant evening visiting her boyfriend, Ricky Max Rush. The pair
played a few games of backgammon and then watched Starsky and
Hutch on television. It was around 10:30 when Ricky drove Tana
back to her apartment. Here, she enacted another of her recent
security routines, asking Ricky to enter the unit ahead of her to do
a sweep. Aware that Tana took this stuff seriously, Ricky indulged

her, going through each room before announcing that the place was clear, and it was safe to enter. He then kissed his girlfriend goodnight and departed. They both had to work in the morning.

Tana Woolley was a responsible young woman who seldom, if ever, missed a day of work. So when she failed to show up on the morning of Wednesday, October 25, failed even to call in sick, her boss was immediately concerned. He called Tana's mom, Helen, to apprise her of the situation. Helen agreed that it was unlike Tana and decided to drive to her daughter's apartment to check on her. That would turn out to be the most traumatic event of her life.

Entering through the unlocked front door, Helen was immediately confronted by the gruesome sight of her daughter's semi-nude body lying across the bed with her head hanging over the edge and her long blonde locks draped towards the floor. Tana was naked from the waist down, save for a long athletic sock on one of her feet. Its twin was twisted around her neck, twisted tight. It was immediately obvious that she wasn't breathing. Helen backed out of the apartment and went to call the police.

Two important pieces of evidence were retrieved from Tana Woolley's apartment that day. The first was the murder weapon, Tana's own sock that had been used to strangle her. The second was a bedspread marked by a stain that turned out to be semen. It seemed obvious that the motive for the killing was to cover up a sexual assault and this would be confirmed by the autopsy. Tana had been raped. Sometime during the night, someone had forced the lock on her front door and entered, attacking the young woman in her bed. Time of death was put at around 11:30 p.m. Neighbors reported hearing a scream at that time.

Rosamond, California falls under the jurisdiction of the Kern County Sheriff's Department, which has a substation in the town. This is a small force unused to dealing with an investigation of this magnitude. Certainly, the Woolley family was dissatisfied with the effort being expended in finding their daughter's killer. Within two weeks of Tana's funeral, they decided to bring in their own investigator.

Lou McNab was a veteran P.I. He started by going back to the source, interviewing residents of Tana's building. Here, he picked up a detail that the overworked Kern County detectives had somehow neglected to follow up. Several of the female tenants told him that he should be speaking to Larry Hazlett, who they described as the "building creep."

Taking their advice, McNab sat down with Hazlett and asked if he, as Tana's neighbor, had seen or heard anything. Hazlett said no. He'd had to make a trip to the store, he said, and was away from his apartment at the time that other residents reported hearing the scream. However, it wasn't Hazlett's words that interested McNab, but his demeanor. The detective reckoned himself a good judge of character. He came away from the interview convinced that he'd identified Tana's killer. Now, all he had to do was prove it.

But Larry Hazlett quit town a long time before Lou McNab was able to gather the requisite proof. Indeed, McNab would never find the evidence he needed to back up his suspicions. And neither would the Kern County Sheriff's Department. Overworked and under-resourced, its investigators moved on to more solvable crimes. Tana Woolley's case might easily have slipped through the cracks but for the pressure put on the police by her family. Helen Woolley never let up. She phoned at least once a month, asking for updates, wanting to know if there was more that could be done.

Despite those efforts, there was no progress in the case over the next five years. In 1983, the Sheriff's Department asked the FBI for help in compiling a profile of the offender. This hypothesized that the killer was late teens to early 20s. It suggested that this was an interracial crime. The killer was probably black. He'd likely tried to convince the victim to have sex and had become angry when she'd rejected him. Parts of this profile would turn out to be accurate. Other parts, like the age of the offender, were wrong. In the end, the profile did little to help solve the crime. The case was cold.

Twenty years passed. In 1999, with still no hint of a resolution, Tana's sister, Taryn, took over from her mother in applying pressure to the police. Taryn put together an album, containing photos of Tana, family snapshots, poems written by her dead sister. This she handed to the detective currently assigned to the case. She wanted him to see her as a person, loved and missed by her family, not just as a name on a case file.

And it worked. Sgt Chris Speer agreed to review the case file, where he found a request for a fingerprint check on a man named

Larry Hazlett. Speer hadn't heard the name before, but he soon discovered that Hazlett was a man with a checkered past. He was a registered sex offender, convicted of misdemeanor molestation of a minor. There were also arrests for drugs, for burglary, for kidnapping.

But what really drew Speer's attention were the four arrests for rape. On each of these occasions, Hazlett had walked, after the victims decided not to bring the matter to court. When it came to the law, Hazlett seemed to be living a charmed life. He'd gotten away with rape on at least four occasions. Speer wondered if he'd also gotten away with murder.

One thing would confirm or allay this suspicion. The police had the semen sample from the crime scene and needed to compare it to Hazlett's DNA. Speer got a warrant and then visited Hazlett at his home in Sacramento. He expected some reluctance from Hazlett and was surprised when he submitted willingly to the swab. So willingly, in fact, that Speer began to question his instincts. Perhaps he was wrong about Hazlett.

The DNA test, however, would deliver a match. The semen stain on Tana Woolley's bedspread had come from Hazlett. But now, Speer had to tread carefully. It is a common ploy for killers to try and explain away the presence of semen by claiming that sex had been consensual and that the victim had been alive when they left. This kind of assertion is difficult, if not impossible, to disprove. If Speer erred in his line of questioning, the case might well be sunk.

In December 2002, Speer and Detective Joe Hicks visited Hazlett
again at his home. The officers had rehearsed their strategy
beforehand. Hicks would take the lead. Initially, he said nothing
about the DNA match, instead asking Hazlett about his
relationship with Tana Woolley. Hazlett said that there wasn't one.
He didn't know the woman, had never spoken to her, had never
been inside her apartment, certainly had never had sex with her.
"And you never killed her?" Hicks asked. To this, Hazlett
responded with an almost puritanical, "Good heavens, no!"

It was at this point that Hicks dropped the bomb. "Would it change
your story if I told you that the Kern County District Attorney's lab
found biological evidence of you being present at the crime
scene?"

"That's a goddam lie!" Hazlett responded angrily. He then clammed
up and refused to say anything more without a lawyer present.

And Hazlett would maintain that stance right into the trial, where
he entered a not guilty plea. It is hard to understand how he
thought he could beat the rap with all the evidence against him.
This included the harrowing testimony of the four women he'd
raped, as well as additional DNA evidence. The lab had found it on
the sock that had been used to strangle Tana. Hazlett had pulled
this tight around the young woman's throat, maintaining his grip
while her life ebbed away. It required considerable pressure, even
for a powerfully built man like Hazlett. In the process, he'd left
behind skin cells, embedded in the fabric. Now, nearly three
decades later, those telltale cells would damn him as a killer.

In the end, it took the jury just 90 minutes to find Larry Hazlett guilty of murder with special circumstances. He was sentenced to death and shipped off to San Quentin's death row. In March 2019, the State of California placed a moratorium on judicial executions meaning that Hazlett will escape the fate he deserves. He will not die by the needle. He will, however, die behind bars.

Rot in Hell

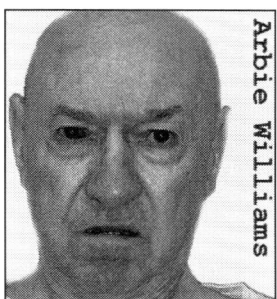

On a sunny afternoon in September 1982, Linda Strait took a stroll to her local Safeway to buy a hair perm kit. She never returned. Linda was just 15 years old on the day she disappeared. She was a sophomore at North Central High in Spokane, Washington, a member of the school basketball team, a talented musician who played the flute. She enjoyed roller skating and video games. She was close to her mom and enjoyed hanging out with her cousins, John and Theresa Milla. She certainly wasn't the kind of girl to go off somewhere without letting anyone know.

And yet, Linda was missing, disappeared along a route that was barely 500 yards either way, passing through a well-populated area, in broad daylight. How was this possible?

That was the conundrum that the Spokane police were left to answer after Linda's parents reported her missing that evening. A search was launched right away and would be resolved within 24 hours, tragically so. A fisherman came across Linda's body the next day, washed up on the bank of the Spokane River near Plantes Ferry Park. An autopsy determined that the teenager had been raped and strangled. An embroidered pillowcase was found near the scene and checked into evidence. Sent to the lab, it tested positive for semen. Back in 1982, that wasn't the case breaker that it might be today.

Spokane PD threw everything it had at the investigation, putting officers on the street to question everyone who lived or worked along the route Linda had taken. Surely, someone must have seen something. Astonishingly, no one had. The case dominated local news media for weeks with Linda's stepfather, George Ragland, appearing on television multiple times to appeal for anyone with information to come forward. If anyone had seen or heard anything, they failed to alert the authorities. The police would interview nearly 1,000 people over the course of the inquiry, including several potential suspects. None of the leads panned out.

Eight months passed. On a May afternoon in 1983, two eight-year-olds were walking along the sidewalk outside Trent Elementary School when a man called them over to his car. He said that he had dropped his keys somewhere inside the vehicle and asked if they would help him look for them. The girls agreed and got into the car. In doing so, they stepped into a nightmare. The man immediately started the engine and drove off with the girls trapped inside. He took them to a wooded area where he ordered them to take off their clothes. One of the girls complied. The other took the opportunity to sprint away and escape.

For the child who remained, there would be an hours-long ordeal of pain and terror. The eight-year-old was repeatedly raped by her abductor, then throttled into unconsciousness and dumped in the undergrowth. Apparently, the rapist believed that she was dead. He was wrong. This brave little girl later revived and managed to stagger from the woods and find help. It was through her testimony that Arbie Dean Williams was eventually caught, convicted, and sent to prison. The world was a safer place with him behind bars.

In the meantime, the investigation into Linda Strait's murder was faltering. What little evidence the police had, had been worked and reworked, each time coming up empty. For a time, the police considered the possibility that Linda might have fallen victim to the Green River Killer, the still unidentified serial killer who was cutting a swathe of death across the Spokane area. But that particular psycho preyed primarily on prostitutes and runaways. Linda did not fit his victim profile and likely had not encountered him. The identity of her killer remained an unfathomable mystery and seemed likely to remain so.

However, the Spokane Police Department wasn't giving up. In 1990, it decided to take another run at the case. Clues were scant but investigators did have two workable leads, both related to the pillowcase found at the scene. First, they sent the sperm sample to the lab hoping that a profile could be lifted and matched to a suspect. Unfortunately, the fledgling technology of DNA profiling was not up to the task at the time.

Next, the police homed in on the pillowcase itself. The embroidery pattern was unusual. Perhaps someone would recognize it. It was time to appeal to the public once again. Pictures of the pillowcase were shown across various media, in the hope of jarring someone's memory. No one came forward, not even when Linda's parents put up a $10,000 reward for information.

Eight more years went by without progress in the investigation. For Linda's mom, Donna, this was a difficult time, a time of heartache and tears and impotent anger. Her beloved daughter was gone, taken long before her time. Worse still, Donna had to live with the knowledge that Linda, her Linda, the beautiful child she'd birthed and raised, had died helpless and alone, in terror and pain. And the monster who had committed this atrocity was still out there, living his life, probably hurting other children. It was more than a mother could bear.

And yet, Donna remained determined to see justice done. While those around her wavered and tacitly accepted that Linda's killer had gotten away with it, Donna never doubted. She'd made a promise to herself. She would live long enough to confront her daughter's killer. "I refuse to die until that happens," she'd say. In 1998, she moved a step closer to that goal.

That was when the case file landed on the desk of Spokane County Sheriff's Office detective Tim Hines. Hines had a significant advantage over those who had previously worked the case. DNA technology had advanced exponentially during the interceding years. Samples that had been unworkable in the past, might well deliver a result now.

However, the process was still prohibitively expensive. It would take four years before the Spokane County Board of Commissioners eventually approved the budget for expanded testing. Linda Strait's case was one of the first to qualify. The semen sample had become partially degraded during the long years it had spent in an evidence room. It was still good enough to return a match.

Arbie Dean Williams, the abductor, rapist, and attempted murderer of eight-year-olds was coming to the end of his sentence at that time. He was sitting in his cell at McNeil Island Correctional Institute, probably contemplating his impending freedom, and what he would do with it. Nothing good, is the likely answer. Then Williams was called to an interview room where a stern-faced detective waited with new accusations, accusations of a crime even more serious than the ones for which he was now serving time.

Williams was done and he knew it. His DNA at the scene proved that he was a killer, and no jury was going to say different. Backed into a corner, he asked for a deal. He'd plead guilty to second-degree murder and accept a 20-year term. He was doing it, he said, to spare his victim's family the trauma of a trial.

Of course, Williams wasn't offering his plea for any reason that involved consideration for others. The man was incapable of such empathy. He was doing it for himself, looking to obtain a reduced sentence. Nonetheless, a deal was struck. Williams appeared for sentencing on July 31, 2006, and entered the guilty plea that he'd agreed to.

However, the killer was about to come in for a rude shock. Williams had been keen to keep the details of his evil deeds out of the public arena. The judge had other ideas. As he began his summation it was clear that he intended describing the crime for the record. Williams quickly interjected, saying that he wanted to withdraw his guilty plea. "You are free to do so," the judge informed him, "But your confession stands." In response, Williams withdrew his objection.

Now, Williams would have to run the gauntlet of victim's impact statements. Among those was a surprise witness. The little girl he'd raped when she was an eight-year-old was now an adult. She faced Williams across the courtroom and told him that it was destiny that she had survived his attempt to end her life. "I was meant to go on and point you out and put you away because you wouldn't have stopped," she said. "To come in contact with you is to lose a part of your soul. Not even death is good enough for you." She then demanded that he face her, taunting him when he refused. "You can't look at me now, can you?" Williams kept his eyes directed firmly at the floor.

Finally, it was the turn of Donna Ragland. Donna had always sworn that she would live long enough to face down her daughter's killer. Now, she described to him the beautiful young woman whose life he'd so callously ended. "She was the light of my life," Donna said, holding back tears. Then she steeled herself to deliver a final rebuke. "I think you are the scum of the earth," she said. "I hope you rot in hell."

Unfortunately, this would not be the last time that Linda's loved ones would have to be in the same room as Arbie Dean Williams. In 2019, having served 13 years of his 20-year sentence, he was up for parole. Now 75 years old, Williams cut a pathetic figure as he played the frail old man card to the hilt. The parole board wasn't buying it and sent him back to Clallam Bay Corrections Center, where he will remain for at least seven more years. It may well end up being longer than that. Once Williams completes his criminal sentence, the State of Washington has the option of retaining him under a civil sentence as a habitual sexual predator. He may see out the rest of his days behind bars.

Fourteen, Going on Psycho

It is not often that Scottsdale, Arizona finds itself at the center of national attention. But that is what happened in the summer of 1978. A Hollywood star had been found battered to death in his Scottsdale apartment. Bob Crane was the lead actor on the popular TV show, Hogan's Heroes. His death would fill column inches and dominate news bulletins for weeks to come, revealing lurid details about his personal life. Crane, it seemed, had been a connoisseur of kinky sex. A friend and fellow debauchee, John Henry Carpenter, would be arrested for the murder but was ultimately acquitted. The general consensus is that Carpenter did it. The case remains officially unsolved.

Amid all this star-spangled furor, the disappearance of a 14-year-old went all but unnoticed by the media and was barely investigated by the police. Greg Holman was a popular kid in his Scottsdale neighborhood, the kind of kid that others gravitated toward. Greg had a large circle of friends. He could handle himself in a fight and often stepped in to protect younger kids. He was still a teenager, though, and not above sowing some wild oats. Like most in his peer group, he'd chug a beer when he could lay his hands on one. He was also a regular user of marijuana.

Also living in Greg Holman's neighborhood at the time was a boy named Jon Benson, a bulky 14-year-old with a bad reputation. Jon was a thug and a bully, frequently in trouble and regularly bailed out by his wealthy parents. He was a spoilt brat who had wanted for nothing in his life. Well, at least nothing that money could buy. What Jon really wanted was to be popular like Greg Holman.

Jon's popularity, though, was bought and paid for. He could often be found trying to coax the neighborhood kids to hang out at his house. Since his parents were often away, giving them the run of the place, many took him up on the offer. However, it was another feature of the property that made it popular with the youngsters. In its yard was a large grotto, popularly known as "The Fort." This was where the kids would assemble to drink and smoke pot.

Hanging out at The Fort, though, carried some risk. Word on the streets was that Jon Benson was a sexual predator. The rumors were well-founded. Benson had already lured several young boys into the hole and molested them. These stories had yet to surface in the adult sphere, but the kids all knew about them. Greg Holman certainly knew, and he wasn't going to let it stand. In September of 1978, he assembled a group of friends to ambush Benson and teach him a lesson. Jon would suffer a beating at their hands. He would also be relieved of his cash and his stash of marijuana.

Jon Benson never reported the assault. Most likely, he was afraid of what would surface should the police start looking into the matter. Actually, Benson seemed to take the whole thing in his stride. Just a few weeks after the incident, he and Greg Holman were seen walking the streets of the neighborhood together. This shocked those who saw them. The two of them had never been close. If anything, they'd always been sworn enemies.

So, what was this about? Had the beating persuaded Jon to change his ways? Had he extended an olive branch? Had Greg accepted? No one knew the answers to those questions, and no one ever would. Greg Holman was seen entering the Benson property with his new friend on the afternoon of October 8, 1978. After that, Greg Holman disappeared.

Greg was reported missing, of course, but Scottsdale PD brushed off his parents' concerns and labeled him a runaway. They were four months into the Bob Crane murder investigation at this time. They had their hands full running down leads and dealing with media inquiries. Such a high-profile investigation can quickly swamp a small force. A 14-year-old runaway did not register very high up on their priority list.

Detectives did at least question Jon Benson, who had been seen with Greg on the day he went missing. Benson said that they'd hung out for a while and that Greg had then left. He hadn't seen him since. With no reason to disbelieve him, the police let it go at that. It would be three years before they questioned Greg again. At that time, the now 17-year-old Benson was asked to take a polygraph. He failed. Shortly after, Benson's dad, Arnold, hired a backhoe and filled in the hole in his backyard. The Fort was no more.

For those of a more conspiratorial mindset, the timing of this maintenance work might seem suspicious. Why now, after all these years, had Arnold Benson decided to fill in the hole? Why now, when the police were taking a renewed interest in the Holman disappearance? Why now, when his son was being questioned? Might The Fort hold some secret that the Benson family wanted to conceal? Might it hold the answer to a mystery? Perhaps. Or maybe Arnold had just grown tired of having an unsightly crater in the middle of his yard.

In any case, the investigation quickly faltered. Greg Holman's family would remain without answers for another decade, until 1992. Then, a new set of investigators took on the case and learned for the first time of The Fort. The teen hangout might have been a part of local folklore, but no police officer had ever heard of it until now. The Benson family had since sold the house, but the new owners were happy for the police to evacuate the area if it would bring some closure to the Holman family. In December of 1992, the dig team moved in. Within a matter of days, it had recovered a headless, handless skeleton. Greg Holman had been found.

Or had he? While everyone in the neighborhood was certain that this was Greg, the police could not make that assumption. They would need more concrete evidence before making an identification. The absence of the head made that difficult since there were no teeth to compare to dental records. DNA was the other option, but the technology was still quite primitive back in the early 90s and was not up to the task. The discovery of the skeleton had offered the hope of long-sought answers. Instead, it left the police and the Holman family with more questions. Greg's parents would go to their graves never knowing what had happened to their son. His mother suffered considerable mental anguish towards the end of her life. Her last words were to wonder what had become of her beloved boy. This is the havoc that killers wreak on families.

The Holman case was back in limbo and would remain so until 2006. That was when Scottsdale PD formed its cold case unit. Greg Holman had now been missing for almost three decades. The skeletal remains had been buried at Green Acres Mortuary for nearly twenty years. One of the first cases targeted by the newly formed unit was this one. The investigative team started by revisiting the site of their earlier dig and excavating the area again, hoping to find more remains or some additional clues. That search came up empty.

Fortunately, the police now had a far more sophisticated toolkit at their disposal. DNA technology had come a long way. The skeletal remains were exhumed and transported to the Maricopa County Medical Examiner's Office, where they were assessed by a forensic anthropologist. They were then brought to the Department of Public Safety for DNA extraction and processing. The results confirmed what everyone already knew. The bones were the mortal remains of Greg Holman.

The identity of Greg Holman's killer wasn't difficult to figure out. Greg had last been seen entering the Benson property in the company of Jon Benson. His bones had been found buried in a hole that had been Jon's primary hangout at that time. Benson's answers during prior investigations had been far from satisfactory. He'd also failed a polygraph. It was time to bring Jon Benson back in for questioning, to squeeze him and see what flowed from there.

Benson wasn't hard to find. He was currently serving a three-and-a-half-year term for the sexual exploitation of a minor. The years, it seemed, had done little to dull his degenerate appetites. Confronted with allegations that he'd murdered Greg Holman, Benson asked for a deal. He had little to lose by taking this path. The murder had been committed when he was just 14 years old. Juvenile guidelines applied. He'd serve minimal time if convicted. In the end, Benson was allowed to plead to manslaughter. In 2008, he received a seven-and-a-half-year sentence. He was released from prison in October of 2014 and is currently a free man, albeit a registered sex offender.

The details of Greg Holman's death remain somewhat of a mystery. We know that Greg was killed on the Benson property and that the murder likely happened inside The Fort. How was he killed? Given that Greg would easily have overcome Jon Benson in a straight-up fight, we must assume that Benson either incapacitated or ambushed him. Perhaps he got Greg drunk or maybe he struck him from behind with some heavy object. Since Benson isn't saying, we don't know. Either way, here we have a 14-year-old who is already a serial rapist, committing the cold-blooded murder of another child. Perhaps we should be grateful that Jon Benson did not end up as a serial killer. He certainly had the makings of such a monster.

I'm the One You're Looking For

Quilcene, Washington is a quiet town, a tiny logging community set among the majestic peaks and magnificent forests of Jefferson County, WA. Home to just 500 souls, it is hardly the kind of place where you would expect to find a savage murder. Yet that is exactly what happened on the night of July 26, 1992. The victim was only a child, just 15 years old when she met her brutal end. It was a crime that shocked the residents of Quilcene to their very core. It would continue to haunt them for years to come.

Allison Tornensis had gone to her best friend, Mary Munn, on that Sunday afternoon, promising her mother that she'd call for a ride rather than walk home in the dark. But Myra Tornensis waited in vain for that call to come and subsequent inquiries revealed that Allison wasn't with Mary. That prompted a desperate search by her parents, a fretful night spent worrying about their daughter. When morning came with still no sign of Allison, her dad, Moose, went to the police station and reported her missing. The police then launched a search that continued for five days before its tragic conclusion. Allison was found on August 1, floating face down in the Little Quilcene River. An autopsy revealed that she'd been stabbed 20 times in what appeared to be a frenzied attack.

Initial inquiries filled in some of the details of Allison's last hours. They also raised several perplexing new questions. At around 1 a.m. that afternoon, Allison and Mary had been in a car with two young men when they'd been involved in a minor accident. Shortly after, Allison made a call to some unknown person. Then she and

Mary parted ways. She was next spotted at around 5:45 p.m., standing in front of the Peninsula Food Store in Quilcene, a common hangout for the local kids. No one knows where she was during the intervening hours or where she went after. Another mystery was the clothes Allison was wearing when she was found, which were different from what she'd left home in. Why the change? And where were the clothes she'd been wearing that Sunday afternoon? No one seemed to know.

Then there was perhaps the biggest mystery of all. Why had Allison been killed? This wasn't a sexual assault, and it wasn't a robbery. The teen had nothing worth stealing. Did Allison have any enemies? Police inquiries suggested not. She was just a normal teen, figuring out the world as best as she could. So why had her life been so savagely snuffed out?

One possibility was that this was a random killing, committed by some psychopath. The Pacific Northwest has an unfortunate reputation for producing some of the country's most depraved killers. Ted Bundy, Gary Ridgway, Robert Lee Yates, Jerome Brudos, Dayton Leroy Rogers – all have lived and hunted here, and there are many more. Did Washington have another psycho on its hands? It was a genuine fear. Jefferson County braced itself for another murder. It never came. The killer of Allison Tornensis, whoever he was, had disappeared.

In truth, this was never a case that was likely to be solved. The Jefferson County Sheriff's Office had scant clues and no witnesses. That is not to suggest that the cops did not put in the work. Thousands of hours were expended in the hunt for Allison's killer, with over 200 potential suspects interviewed. The Sherriff's Office also brought in a detective from Seattle, to compile a psychological profile of the killer.

This suggested that their suspect was a man in his early 20s. He would have known Allison, although she likely kept their relationship a secret. He'd be a man with anger management issues, although he'd be able to keep it under wraps and "fit in." The murder was committed by one person, although he may have had help in moving the body. This was the man the Jefferson County authorities should be looking for. It all sounded rather vague. It would end up being remarkably accurate.

The Allison Tornensis case was highly publicized, even getting a slot on America's Most Wanted. That was in 1995, with the murder of now three years old and the cops all out of leads. The broadcast included a reenactment of Allison's last known movements and generated several leads. None of them panned out.

One person would have watched that America's Most Wanted episode with particular interest. His name was Robert Froelich, and he was a Quilcene native, now living in the town of Bremerton, some 44 miles to the south. Froelich was 23 years old and the father of three terribly neglected children. Both he and his wife were meth addicts, and the children frequently went unwashed and unfed. The Froelichs' relationship was one of frequent conflict, with deputies routinely dispatched to their home to break up fights. It seemed only a matter of time before one or both of them overstepped the mark and ended up behind bars. That happened in December of 1994 when Frolich was convicted of 4th-degree assault on his wife and sent down for a short jail term. Things did not improve after his release. In 1995, he admitted to his probation officer that he had trouble controlling his temper and sometimes "went crazy." Just recently, he'd locked his wife out of their home because he knew that he'd have killed her if he'd been able to lay his hands on her.

Froelich and his wife finally divorced in 1997. After that, he tried several times to get clean but relapsed on each occasion and fell into old habits. He was trying again in 2000, while living with his brother in the small town of Gold Beach, Oregon. This time, he'd managed to stay off drugs for six weeks. He was over the hump. The worst of the withdrawal symptoms were behind him. It looked as though he might finally have kicked the habit.

But it wasn't just his drug-riddled body that Robert Froelich needed to cleanse. He'd been carrying something on his conscience for eight long years, something that had haunted him for a long time. Now, without the drugs to dull his pain, he felt that he could keep his secret no longer. Froelich's brother listened in stunned silence as he related the story of a deadly encounter on a July night in 1982. He then convinced Robert that he needed to repeat the story to the police.

Cold cases are seldom solved by confession. Someone who has gotten away with murder for that length of time is usually reluctant to come forward. Time can soothe even the most troubled conscience. But Robert Froelich was ready to tell his story, at least what he could recall of it. His brain had been addled with drugs at the time. Remembrances were somewhat vague.

"I'm the one you're looking for," Froelich said as he sat down with a Gold Beach detective. He then launched into a mishmash of a story, sometimes vague and rambling, sometimes lucid and detailed. According to Froelich, he had driven up from Bremerton that day, to get high with friends back in Quilcene. He was in the middle of a five-day methamphetamine binge at the time. He had never met Allison Tornensis before he was introduced to her at his friend's house. Allison was getting high with the men, according to Froelich, but at some point, she passed out and went to sleep on a bed. Then the men started talking about her, saying that she might rat them out for their drug use.

This kind of paranoia is typical of addicts, but Froelich apparently took it seriously enough to believe that the threat needed to be addressed. After his friends passed out, he fetched a knife from the kitchen and walked with it to the bedroom. Here, he attacked the sleeping teenager, knifing her to death in a frenzied onslaught. According to him, Allison never woke up and never saw it coming. "It has haunted me every day since," he told the detective.

Froelich was vague on a lot of the details. For example, he couldn't say how Allison had ended up in the Little Quilcene River. However, he was explicit in describing the injuries he had inflicted on the girl. It was enough to convince investigators that he was telling the truth. Later, he'd repeat the story to Jefferson County detectives. He did not contest extradition to Washington.

With a signed confession on file, this should have been a simple matter of a guilty plea, a conviction, and a sentence. But Froelich lawyered up once he was in Washington and his counsel convinced him to plead not guilty on account of his drug use. A psychiatric evaluation was ordered, with Froelich found competent to stand trial, if prone to delusional thinking.

Robert Froehlich appeared before the courts in March 2002, charged with second-degree murder. The prosecution was asking for the maximum 20-year term. Defense attorney D.G. Barnhart countered, petitioning for mercy on behalf of his client, stating that the case would never have been solved but for Froehlich turning himself in. "He wasn't running from the law," Barnhart said. "The only thing he was fleeing was his conscience." He was right, of course. The judge imposed the maximum sentence anyway.

That wasn't 20 years, though. It was 16 years, based on sentencing guidelines in place at the time of the murder. Robert Froehlich has since done his time and is now a free man. His current whereabouts are not known.

3,794 Days of Doubt

Arthur Collins

In the town of Auburn, New Hampshire, George Jodoin was a man everyone knew, and most admired. George was the guy who had it all, money, good looks, two successful businesses, a bevy of female admirers. He was an adventurous type, a trained pilot, a skilled sailor, a skydiver. A raconteur and a socialite, George could put anyone at ease in a moment. And, when the occasion warranted it, George could often be persuaded to get on the piano and play a few tunes. As with most things in his life, he had a talent for the instrument. Aside from all this, George Jodoin was a man with a big heart, always willing to support a good cause or to step in and help someone in need. Everyone loved George. Or at least so it seemed until the night of December 26, 2001.

George's good friend, Rick Carron, called on George's house that night to check on him. Rick was somewhat concerned, having been unable to raise the 41-year-old pawnshop owner on the phone. That concern was elevated further when Rick found George's front door unlocked but got no response when he called out his name. An exploration of the house soon unraveled the mystery. The reason George wasn't answering was because George was dead. Someone had crept in during the night and shot him in his sleep.

This was a crime that deeply traumatized the community. Who on earth would have wanted to harm George Jodoin? Had some lethal stranger entered their community? Was he likely to strike again? These very same questions were perplexing the police. Only they didn't believe that this was a stranger killing. The person who'd committed this crime was someone who had known the victim.

Several points of evidence led the police to this conclusion. First, there were no signs of forced entry to the house. The killer had walked in through the front door. Second, there was no obvious motive, no indication of robbery or sexual assault. Third, there was the murder itself. George was found in his bed in the master bedroom. The killer apparently entered while he slept and pumped several bullets into his head and neck. Why so many shots when a single bullet would have done the job? It spoke of a grudge, a vendetta. It spoke of anger.

But this only served to complicate the investigation. No one the police interviewed could imagine anyone harboring any kind of resentment towards George Jodoin. The man had been universally loved. For a time, the police considered the possibility that there might be some romantic intrigue behind the killing. Perhaps George had upset a lover or angered a significant other of one of the many women he dated. Inquiries, though, suggested that this was not the case. George had been a committed bachelor who'd enjoyed playing the field. He made no promises to the women in his life. He'd also been an honorable man who did not get involved with married or attached women.

One interesting clue that did emerge during the canvas of the neighborhood was that gunshots had been heard from the Jodoin property throughout the day. The neighbors had assumed that George was pistol shooting since he had a small target range behind his house. However, the gunfire had long ceased by late afternoon. Then, late at night, they'd heard another series of shots, these fired in quick succession. A short while later, a car was heard driving away in a screech of tires.

No one, unfortunately, had seen the vehicle racing away from the scene. However, neighbors were able to inform the police of three visitors who'd called at the house that day. The first was George's business partner. The second was Ricky Carron, the man who had discovered the body. The third was Arthur Collins, a handyman who did work around George's property and was also known to hang around the pawnshop in his spare time. All three were brought in, questioned, and all denied having anything to do with George's death. Try as they might, investigators could not shake them. Eventually, they had to concede defeat. The case went cold.

Cold cases are seldom resolved in the dramatic way that we see on television. Usually, it comes down to some technological breakthrough, most commonly involving DNA. Since all three suspects admitted that they had been with the victim on the day he died, that was not an option here. If the police were going to solve this crime, they'd have to do it the old-school way, by getting the suspects in a room, sweating them, and hoping that one of them cracked. In 2011, ten years after the murder, they decided to do just that.

The only suspect who we need to focus on here is Arthur Collins, the burly handyman with the pudding bowl haircut. Back in 2001, Collins had provided an alibi for the time of the murder, an alibi that investigators had been unable to crack. Now, they revisited that testimony, asking Collins to reprise what he'd told them ten years earlier. Soon Collins trapped himself in a contradiction. Then, he tried to explain himself out of that corner and only succeeded in talking himself deeper into trouble. Before long, he was floundering. That was when he suddenly blurted out a stunning confession.

Collins now admitted that he'd been present when George Jodoin was killed, although he denied pulling the trigger. According to Collins, he'd brought a friend to George's house that day and it was this man who'd committed the murder. Collins was then asked to call his friend and to get him to incriminate himself on tape. He agreed and made the call with recording equipment capturing every word. However, it was soon clear that the man wasn't going to confess to murder. He seemed perplexed by the leading questions Collins was putting to him and eventually, he hung up. Collins was then asked to take a polygraph. He agreed and failed. That was when the detectives knew they had him.

Lie detector tests are not admissible in a court of law, of course, but they do provide leverage during an interrogation. Collins was brought in for another round of questions and this time the detectives really turned up the heat. Eventually, the handyman cracked and admitted that he'd killed his friend and employer. He'd done it, he said, because George had made a pass at him.

Arthur Collins was brought to trial at Rockingham County Superior Court in Brentwood, New Hampshire. A plea deal allowed him to plead to the lesser charge of second-degree murder and to accept a prison term of 30 years to life. Over two dozen of George Jodoin's relatives were present to watch his killer go down. Several offered victim impact statements, describing the huge hole that George's absence had left in their lives.

And it wasn't just George's family who'd been affected. Rick Carron had lost a cherished friend and had remained a suspect in his murder for over 10 years. The stresses of the investigation were such that they'd resulted in the breakup of his family. Now, at last, he'd been vindicated. Rick brought a sign to court that day and held it up at the end of the trial. It read: "3,794 days of doubt."

Arthur Collins is currently incarcerated at the Northern New Hampshire Correctional Facility in Berlin, New Hampshire. One of his victim's relatives expressed the hope that he will die behind bars but there is a good chance, if he behaves himself and remains in good health, that he will one day be free. He is eligible for parole in 2042.

One question remains. What was it that motivated Arthur Collins to cold-bloodedly murder a man who considered him a friend, a man who'd been nothing but good to him? Collins' explanation of a sexual advance can be readily dismissed. George Jodoin was clearly heterosexual. And even if we are to entertain the idea that he propositioned Collins, we know that George was asleep in bed when he was killed. This wasn't a murder committed in a moment of outrage. This was an assassination.

The suggestion offered by the police is that the murder had nothing to do with sex and that Collins' true motive was robbery. But if that was the case then why wasn't the house ransacked? Why was nothing taken? Did Collins intend robbery but lose his nerve after committing the murder? It's possible.

However, there is a third possibility. I would suggest that Collins was obsessed with George Jodoin. This isn't a stretch when we consider how much time he spent hanging around George, a man who was ostensibly his employer. Proximity most likely made him envious of George's lifestyle, his wealth, his looks, his talent, his success with women. He wanted George's life and since he was never going to have it, he decided that George shouldn't either. Five bullets proved the equalizer. This was an act of pure vindictiveness.

Here Comes Trouble

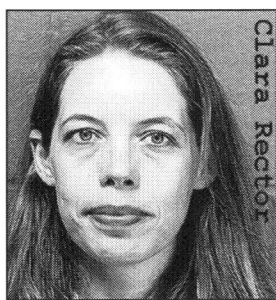

All her life, Clara Rector had been a troubled soul. Born in 1976 in California, Clara was raised in a home so dysfunctional that she was eventually removed from her family and placed in foster care. That would be a godsend for Clara who was soon adopted by a new family and moved to the Lake of the Ozarks. The rest of her childhood passed without significant trauma. She graduated high school and by age 19 was already a married woman. However, fate was not yet done with tossing curveballs in Clara's direction. On the day that she found out she was pregnant with her first child, her husband was killed in a car crash.

The death was devastating to Clara, sending her into a steep downward spiral. She began using drugs and soon hooked up with a fellow user, a man named Jason Rector. Somewhere in the haze of their drug-addled existence, Jason proposed, and Clara said yes. But Jason got clean after the wedding and Clara did not. She continued using, even through two more pregnancies and the birth of two children. And when Jason didn't want to get high with her anymore, she went looking for someone who would. She found him in Tommy Hope.

Tommy was 19 years older than Clara but, in other ways, they had much in common. Like Clara, he was a product of the foster system. Born in Texas in 1955, Tommy was raised with two other siblings and was abused and severely neglected during his childhood. Often, his parents would disappear for days at a time, leaving the children to fend for themselves. Eventually, the state stepped in and took them away.

But for Tommy, there would be no happy ending, no caring family to step in and ease his suffering. He'd spend his entire childhood being shifted from one foster home to another, suffering abuse and neglect in several of them. This continued until he was old enough to set off on his own. With few options available, he joined the military, serving for several years before earning an honorable discharge. After that, he bounced from place to place, working at odd jobs to earn his keep. By his early 40s, he'd landed in Camdenton, Missouri, a small town near the Lake of the Ozarks. Here, he decided to put down roots.

Life had dealt Tommy Hope a rough hand, but Tommy was determined to play it as best he could. Despite his many traumas, Tommy was a personable individual, who made friends easily. He was soon a familiar face on the Camdenton bar scene, with plenty of drinking buddies along for the ride. His choice of stimulants also went to harder substances than alcohol. Tommy always kept a small cache of cocaine, marijuana, and methamphetamine, in his house. These attracted a different category of friend, people like Clara Rector.

It is uncertain how Tommy and Clara met but Camdenton is a small town and like-minded individuals will find each other. Soon Clara was sneaking out of her home at night, to get high with Tommy and swap stories about their hurtful upbringings. Neither the 19-year age gap nor Clara's marital status proved an impediment to attraction, and they started sleeping together.

Word of this affair inevitably reached Jason and he paid a visit to Tommy, threatening him with violence if he continued seeing his wife. That had precisely the opposite effect to what he wanted. Rather than give up her steady supply of drugs, Clara moved out of her family home and took up with Tommy. This tense situation continued for several months before Clara heeded her husband's desperate pleas and agreed to go into rehab. She emerged in late 2003, all cleaned up and determined to give her marriage another shot.

But Clara's ride on the sobriety wagon lasted barely a few turns of the wheel. She was soon sneaking out to get high with Tommy. Then the whole melodrama played out again. Jason showed up on Tommy's doorstep all spit and fire; Tommy told him to go to hell. Clara was an adult, and he wasn't her master. She could do as she pleased.

It was now April of 2004. In Camdenton life went on, moving at its typically sedate pace. In the city's drinking holes, the regulars still met, to chug beers and cocktails and exchange war stories. Only, something was different. Tommy Hope, so often the life of the party, hadn't been seen for several days. His friends were getting worried about him.

And so, at around 6:30 on the morning of April 28, 2004, Cindy Christenson and Brian Norton went to check on Tommy. They arrived to find his place in darkness and securely locked. Knocking on the door brought no response. Neither did calling out Tommy's name. Eventually, Cindy decided to squeeze through a small bathroom window.

This was how Tommy Hope was found, dead on the floor of his living room in a pool of blood. Seeing him there, Cindy immediately fled the house. She and Brian then went to the nearby home of a friend and called 911. "He's lying face down," Cindy told the dispatcher. "There's blood on the carpet and stuff too, right around his face area. Like, you know, he's been bleeding from his head."

Tommy Hope had died in a vicious knife attack, suffering eight deep wounds to his neck, torso, and left arm. The medical examiner determined that he'd been dead for three to four days, meaning that he'd been killed on the night of April 24 or the morning of April 25. Luminol uncovered bloody footprints leading to a window, while prints on the window frame indicated where the killer had exited the home. Who had done this? The police had a pretty good idea. Jason Rector had threatened to kill Tommy many times in the past.

And Jason hardly helped his cause when he sat down to be interviewed by detectives and told them, "I'm glad he's dead." However, he followed this up by denying any involvement in the murder, insisting that he'd been home all night with his wife. That was hardly a cast iron alibi, but the physical evidence backed up his claims of innocence. The bloody footprints were too small to be his and the prints on the sill weren't a match. Jason was off the hook and the investigation was already in trouble. Ultimately, it would come up short. No one was arrested nor indicted. A killer walked free.

Nine years passed. In April 2013, the Camden County Sheriff's Office was asked to investigate a rather less serious crime. Pastor Jerry Sousley of the Camdenton Bible Baptist Church had a stalker. According to Sousley, he was being sexually harassed by one of his parishioners. The female stalker had been sending him inappropriate messages. She'd also been putting notes on his car windshield and had left a journal in his office, detailing her sexual fantasies about him.

The pastor had tried reasoning with the woman, explaining that he was happily married and that adultery was a sin. But that had only made her angry. Now she was threatening to "destroy him." Sousley had every reason to take the threat seriously. He was convinced that the woman was capable of violence and might harm him or his family. He knew this because she'd once admitted to him during a counseling session that she'd killed a man.

The woman in question was Clara Rector and the murder she'd described to Pastor Sousley sounded a lot like the killing of Tommy Hope. Clara was taken into custody on April 21, 2013, and charged with harassment and stalking. Detectives who had worked the Hope murder were then brought in to question her. Initially, they stuck to the harassment charge but then they suddenly switched tack and started asking about Tommy. This was designed to catch her off guard, but Clara barely blinked. After taking a moment to gather her thoughts, she was talking, confessing to a murder that had gone unsolved for nine years.

According to Clara, she had snuck out of her house that night, after Jason fell asleep. She'd headed for Tommy's place where she hoped to get high. However, Tommy wouldn't let her in, saying that he had no drugs on the premises. Convinced that he was lying, Clara crept in through a window and confronted him. Tommy then agreed to share the small amount of cocaine he had with her.

But that barely scratched the itch and now Clara was getting agitated. She started accusing Tommy of holding out on her. Tommy, though, wasn't interested in a fight. He turned and started walking away. That was when Clara picked up a knife from the table, jumped on his back, and drew the blade across his throat.

"I started like, 'I hate you. I hate you!'" she told the detectives. "He was standing there against the wall and he's like, 'You know, I think you're killing me, I think I'm dying.' Then he just fell over."

With Tommy bleeding out on the ground, Clara lifted his wallet and then climbed back through the window, carrying the murder weapon with her. She arrived home covered in blood and found Jason awake and waiting for her. Considering the circumstances, he seems to have been remarkably composed. After listening to his wife's story, he took control of the situation, helping her dispose of the murder weapon and other incriminating evidence. They'd then spent some time getting their story straight, each providing an alibi to the other.

Clara and Jason Rector were arrested on April 24, 2013, nine years to the day from Tommy Hope's murder. Clara was charged with first-degree murder, Jason with felony evidence tampering. His charges would later be dropped since the statute of limitations had run out. For Clara, though, there was no such escape. The statute never runs out on murder. She entered a guilty plea at trial and was sentenced to 15 years in prison. Clara Rector is currently held at Chillicothe Correctional Center. She is eligible for parole in 2024 when she will be 47 years old.

Chasing Shadows

Jerome Barrett

In the city of Nashville, Tennessee, about 10 miles south of downtown, is a suburb called Green Hills, an upper-middle-class enclave of leafy, tree-lined streets and solid, brick houses with neatly trimmed lawns. This is a neighborhood out of an idealized America, a place where neighbors still exchange greetings and where cars give way to morning joggers on the street. Crime is rare here and has always been so. It might therefore surprise you to learn that one of the city's most traumatic events took place right here on these tranquil boulevards. It happened on a chilly February afternoon in 1975.

Marcia Trimble was nine years of age, a fourth grader at the nearby Julia Green Elementary School, a sweet little girl with long blonde locks and a dimpled smile. Marcia lived with her parents, Charles and Virginia, in a three-bedroom ranch-style house on Copeland Drive. She was a lively, outgoing girl, active in the local Girl Scout troop, which she loved. Early on the evening of February 25, Marcia told her mom that she was going to deliver some Girl

Scout cookies to a neighbor. Virginia told her to wear a coat, but
Marcia said not to worry, she'd be right back.

To our modern sensibilities, the idea of allowing a child so young
to be out alone with darkness falling might seem irresponsible. But
this was the 1970s and this was Green Hills, a place where kids
rode bikes in the street and played pickup games of rounders in
the local park. Others delivered newspapers or went door-to-door
hawking magazine subscriptions. This was a safe place where
everyone looked out for everyone else. Nothing bad could happen
here.

Except, on this day, something bad did happen. On this day, a nine-
year-old child disappeared. Virginia Trimble raised the alarm
almost immediately she realized that her daughter was late in
getting home. That sparked a search of the surrounding area, with
neighbors rallying to Virginia's aid. By the time the police were
alerted, the whole neighborhood was in uproar. The cops then
brought additional manpower to the fore, including a K-9 unit with
a team of bloodhounds. Things escalated from there, with the State
Police and then the FBI getting involved. Despite this massive
effort, there was no trace of the little girl over the days and weeks
that followed.

Right from the start, the police had a theory. They believed that
Marcia had been taken by someone living in the neighborhood.
This made sense. In such a close-knit community, a stranger would
stand out. The cops further extrapolated their hypothesis to
suggest that the perpetrator might be a juvenile. Again, this was a
rational conclusion. Marcia had disappeared in the early evening

when most adult males would just be returning from work. This theory, that a teenager had snatched Marcia, would receive further validation when a 15-year-old came forward to tell what he knew.

The boy's name was Jeffrey Womack, and he lived just a short distance from the Trimble residence. According to Jeffrey, Marcia had knocked on his door that evening, trying to sell him some cookies. He'd sent her away telling her that he did not have any money. The timing of this encounter would have made him one of the last people to see the little girl alive.

And that detail was not lost on the police. Jeff Womack might have thought that he was being a good citizen by sharing his information but he soon found himself the prime suspect. A detective ordered him to empty his pockets. What he placed on the counter attracted the immediate attention of everyone present – a roll of pennies, a five-dollar bill, and a condom.

"I thought you said you didn't have any money," the detective demanded. Jeff responded that he'd only told Marcia that so that he could send her away without seeming rude. The officer then wanted to know why he had a condom in his pocket. He said it was because he was in a sexual relationship with a local woman. That did not go down well. Here was a sexually precocious teen who was possibly the last person to see a missing nine-year-old before she inexplicably vanished. It fit the police theory exactly.

The police would expend much of their investigative effort on Jeffrey Womack. They continued to press the teenager for answers until his mother got a lawyer and that lawyer instructed the boy not to respond to their questions. It was sound advice given the circumstances. It only made the cops more convinced that Jeffrey was their man. In the meantime, the search for Marcia went on. It would endure for 33 days during which her disappearance dominated conversations all over Nashville. All the while, Charles and Virginia Trimble hunkered down in their home, avoiding the news crews camped outside and praying for their daughter's safe return. On March 30, 1975, those prayers were brutally dashed.

Marcia Trimble was found in a deserted, windowless garage, just 150 yards from her home, her body concealed under a shower curtain and a deflated child's wading pool. The building had been searched before so it remains a mystery why she was not found earlier. Given that she'd been dead for over a month, the body was remarkably well-preserved. The cold weather had delayed decomposition. Marcia was fully clothed, although there was evidence of sexual assault, with semen stains found on her blouse and pants. The medical examiner also found semen inside the child's vagina, although there was no indication that she'd been raped. The killer had either masturbated over her corpse, or he'd ejaculated before he could penetrate her. Cause of death was determined to be strangulation. Marcia had a fractured hyoid bone. The killer had left her on the ground amidst a scatter of Girl Scout cookies. He'd walked away with the money she'd earned selling cookies that day.

Many missteps were made during this investigation, including the mishandling of biological evidence which led to degradation of the samples. This would later be a significant impediment once DNA technology became available. That, however, lay far in the future. For now, the police remained obsessed with Jeffrey Womack, even launching an undercover operation to try and coax a confession out of him.

In 1977, the now 17-year-old Womack was working as a busboy in a restaurant, when he was befriended by another employee. Unbeknownst to Jeff, his new pal was an undercover cop. The officer tried hard to get an admission out of him but failed. Womack was also asked to take two polygraph tests during this time. He passed both. The authorities eventually charged him with Marcia Trimble's murder in 1980, but it was never going to stick. There was not a shred of evidence linking him to this terrible crime. The charges were soon dismissed.

Years went by, years without closure for the Trimble family, years during which the cloud of suspicion continued to hang over Jeffrey Womack. During that time, there were significant advancements in crime detection technology, most notably in the field of DNA profiling. The Metro Nashville Police Department took advantage of this discovery by obtaining samples from 96 male residents of Green Hills, including Jeff Womack. These were tested against the semen samples lifted from the crime scene, but the results were inconclusive. The sample was degraded and the technology was not yet sufficiently advanced to test it. It would be many more years before several factors came together to bring resolution to a 33-year-old case.

In 2008, Metro Nashville detectives were looking into another unsolved murder, the 1975 rape slaying of Vanderbilt University sophomore, Sarah Des Prez. Sarah had been raped and strangled in her off-campus apartment in early February '75. Semen retrieved from the crime scene was now submitted for DNA analysis and returned a match to a habitual sex offender. Jerome Barrett was eventually convicted of the crime and sent to prison for life. His long list of offenses included the brutal rape of a Belmont University student on February 12, barely a week after he killed Sarah Des Prez. That had seen him arrested and sent down for a long prison term.

But Barrett had still been at liberty on February 25, the day that Marcia Trimble was taken. Now, investigators started to wonder. Might he be the man they were looking for, the shadow they'd been chasing all these years?

DNA would provide the answer to that question. Advances in the technology meant that even degraded samples could now be tested with a high degree of success. On December 3, 2007, Nashville television stations reported that DNA recovered from the Trimble crime scene had been matched to a suspect, named as 60-year-old Jerome Sydney Barrett. Six months later, on June 6, 2008, a Davidson County Grand Jury indicted Barrett, charging him with first-degree murder and felony sexual assault.

With the DNA evidence impossible to deny, Barrett admitted murder but denied rape. In fact, he denied any sexual motive at all. He'd been on a mission, he said, to kill "four blue-eyed bitches."

Already serving a life term for the murder of Sarah Des Prez, he received an additional 44 years. He will die behind bars.

Yet, even now, questions remain unanswered about this terrible case. How had Jerome Barrett, a tall and imposing black man, managed to walk the streets of lily-white Green Hills without being noticed? How was he able to snatch a nine-year-old from the street when there were kids shooting hoops in a nearby driveway, parents pulling into drives as they returned from work? How come no one saw or heard anything? Since Barrett offered no explanation at trial, we are left without answers. All we know is this. A killer invaded suburbia on a cold February day and snuffed out the life of a child. That is tragedy enough.

Suspect Zero

His name was Marvin Ray Markle Jr although he preferred to go by
Ziggy. He was 17 years old and a student at Country High School in
Vacaville, California. That was when Ziggy could be bothered to
attend at all. Usually, he preferred hanging out at Will C. Wood
Junior High, trying to impress the younger girls with his tough guy
act. Ziggy seemed particularly interested in Mary Borchers and De
Anna Lynn Johnson, two 14-year-olds who lived in his
neighborhood. Often, he could be seen leaning up against their
locker, doing his best bad boy impersonation. Neither girl was
interested. Ziggy Markle had a reputation as a bully and a
troublemaker. They wanted no part of him.

On the evening of Monday, November 15, 1982, there was a party
on Royal Oaks Drive in Vacaville. De Anna Johnson wanted to
attend but her mom, Ginger, was reluctant to let her go. It was only
after listening to De Anna's constant pleas that Ginger eventually
gave in. There were conditions, though. She was to stick with her
17-year-old brother, Ron, and was to be home by 9:30. With that
agreed, the siblings headed for the party, just seven houses away.

It was 6:00 p.m. when they departed. Only one of them would return.

Teenage house parties are usually raucous and chaotic affairs and this one was no different. It did not take long for Ron and De Anna to be separated as they gravitated to their own groups of friends. They would see each other only fleetingly over the next three-and-a-half hours. As the 9:30 curfew approached, Ron went looking for his sister but couldn't find her. This did not alarm him unduly. He simply assumed that De Anna had gotten bored with the party and decided to head home. It was, after all, just a short walk. She could have covered it in under two minutes.

Only, De Anna wasn't home when he got there and a return trip to the party house failed to locate her or anyone who knew where she might be. That was when alarm bells started to jangle. Within an hour, the police were called in. They continued searching for the missing teen throughout the night.

The mystery of De Anna Johnson's disappearance would be resolved early the next morning. That was when two Southern Pacific Railroad employees were walking the tracks along Elmira Road and discovered the badly beaten body of a young girl lying in the weeds. De Anna had been found within sight of her home. The autopsy revealed that the ninth grader had been strangled, beaten, and bludgeoned to death with a rock.

This was an incredible savage murder, perpetrated against a child who would have had little hope of defending herself. De Anna Johnson stood just five-two and weighed a mere 100 pounds. The amount of force that had been used to end her life was excessive, to say the least. It spoke of an assailant with serious anger issues. Still, De Anna had put up a fight. Skin cells were found under her nails, suggesting that she'd scratched her attacker. And if he had intended to rape her, he hadn't succeeded. She was found fully clothed and had not been violated. De Anna had defended her honor at the cost of her life.

But who would have committed such a terrible atrocity? The obvious place for detectives to start was at the party but this would prove less productive than they hoped. The beer had flowed freely that night and many of the teenage revelers had been inebriated. Quite a few had also been under the influence of stronger stimulants. What the police got was a patchwork of garbled statements, lacking in specifics, often contradictory. The only consistent theme was that no one had seen De Anna leave the party or hanging out with anyone in particular.

Despite this lack of concrete leads, though, there was a name that came up time and again in the investigation. Several of the partygoers and quite a few teens who had not even been there suggested to the police that they should check out Ziggy Markle. Markle had been at the party that night and no one had seen him leave either. Aside from that, he was known for his generally belligerent attitude. A lot of the kids were afraid of him.

And so, Markle was questioned and denied having anything to do with De Anna Johnson's death. It was during this interrogation that officers noticed scratches on his arms and bruising to his hands. Questioned about this, Markle claimed that he'd been involved in an altercation with "some kid in school." He was then asked to produce the clothes and shoes he'd worn to the party. Examination of these items turned up a single drop of blood on one of his boots. Markle said that he didn't know how it got there or who it was from. The droplet proved to be De Anna's blood type but that wasn't enough for an arrest warrant. Markle was allowed to walk. The murder of De Anna Johnson would ultimately go unsolved.

It is now 2001, and Marvin Markle Jr. is living in Biggs, California, occasionally working construction. He still goes by Ziggy and not much else has changed either. He's the same confrontational individual, ready to pick a fight with anyone, provided they appear unwilling or unable to defend themselves. Shirley Pratt was in many ways his ideal victim. She was 41 years of age and living with her drug dealer boyfriend when she disappeared. She was found days later, on October 12, 2001, in the Oroville Wildlife Area in Butte County on October 12, 2001, a bullet hole punched between her eyes.

The condition of the corpse, with the victim's jeans and panties pulled down to her ankles and dried semen on her chest, suggested a sexual motive. However, the autopsy turned up no sign of forced sexual penetration, leading investigators to speculate that she'd resisted her would-be rapist and been killed as a result. Shirley's car was found two miles from the body, burned to the bare metal.

As in the murder of De Anna Johnson, the police had a limited field of suspects to work with. There was also a name that the two murders had in common. Marvin "Ziggy" Markle had been an associate of Shirley Pratt and her boyfriend, Fidel Reyna. There were other similarities, too. Several of Shirley's friends told the police that the man they should be talking to was Marvin Markle. One of them even said that he knew the identity of the killer and wrote down the initials MM. However, he refused to provide a name, saying that he was too afraid.

Marvin Markle wasn't difficult to find. He'd recently handed himself over on an outstanding warrant and was serving a year in prison. What was interesting was the timing. Markle had surrendered to police on the very day that Shirley Pratt's body was found. This is a common ploy by criminals, fessing up to a lesser crime to ride out the storm created by a far more serious one.

And in Markle's case, it worked. Even locked away in prison, he cast a long shadow. Witnesses were afraid to speak out against him, and this pall of fear would end up torpedoing the investigation. Markle saw out his year in prison, walking free in December 2002. Thereafter, the Pratt case went cold. It would be 12 years before the police got a DNA match on the semen from the crime scene. No one was shocked that it was Marvin Markle, no one but Markle himself. He continued to protest his innocence, entering a not guilty plea at trial. Those denials did him no good. Convicted of murder in 2013, he was sentenced to 80 years in prison.

Meanwhile, back in Vacaville, De Anna Johnson had not been forgotten. In 2011, the Vacaville High School Class of '86 held its 25-year reunion. This would have been De Anna's class since she would have attended the school after graduating junior high. The occasion was marked by a poignant moment when Principal Ed Santopadre presented De Anna's uncle, Ed Auld, with her high school diploma. It read: "This certifies that De Anna Lynn Johnson has satisfactorily completed a four-year course of study at Vacaville High School and is therefore awarded this diploma." Nearly 30 years after her death, De Anna had graduated high school.

And the 14-year-old had not been forgotten by the Vacaville Police Department either. Hers had never been a cold case, in the true sense of the term. The file had never been sent to some dusty old cabinet to be locked away and forgotten about. It had been worked actively, with successive generations of detectives periodically scanning the evidence, looking for that one clue that might have eluded them. "This was a puzzle," a Vacaville PD detective told the media. "Some pieces came together in the 80s, some pieces in the 90s, and some in the 2000s. It's not one piece of evidence, it's all the pieces taken together."

But, of course, the most vital piece of this puzzle was the biological material retrieved during the original inquiry, the skin from under De Anna's fingernails, the single drop of blood lifted from Ziggy Markle's boot. In 2016, these eventually delivered the match investigators had been praying for. The skin cells were from Markle. The blood belonged to his victim, De Anna Johnson.

Marvin Markle was arrested in an interview room at Kern Valley State Prison in January 2017 and charged with the first-degree murder of 14-year-old De Anna Johnson. The news was met with relief by De Anna's mom. "Today is a day I thought would never come," Ginger Dimpel told the media. "My daughter died at the hands of a vicious and cowardly murderer. I'm encouraged that the truth will prevail, and justice will finally be done."

The matter has yet to come to trial. In the meantime, Marvin Markle isn't going anywhere.

When Hope Dies

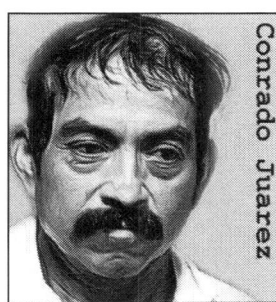

Conrado Juarez

On July 23, 1991, a body was discovered in a wooded area along the Henry Hudson Parkway in upper Manhattan. The remains were those of a child, no older than five years of age. Severely decomposed, the corpse had been trussed up with rope and with the cord from a Venetian blind. The little girl had then been wrapped in garbage bags and crammed inside a navy-blue cooler. She had dark, wavy hair drawn into a ponytail and was believed to be Hispanic. Weighing only 28 pounds, she was severely undernourished. She had also been the victim of sexual abuse. The pathologist believed that she'd been dead for around a month.

Who had committed this terrible crime? Who had raped and murdered a toddler and then discarded her body like trash? The NYPD had no idea, but its officers were determined to find out, to hunt down the perpetrator and bring him to justice. First, though, they'd have to identify the victim. They began that process by issuing an appeal via the media. In all of these articles and broadcasts, this tragic little girl was referred to by the poignant name, Baby Hope.

Regrettably, no one ever came forward to claim Baby Hope. Abused and violated in life, she had been abandoned in death, forgotten, ungrieved. Only, that wasn't entirely true. The officers who worked the case certainly mourned her. So too did anyone who read her tragic story. When, in 1993, it was decided that the remains should be buried, the NYPD put up the money for a plot and a casket. Two hundred mourners showed up at the public funeral, many of them in uniform. One of the investigating officers read a moving eulogy and many tears were shed for this little girl who none of the congregation had known in life. The child's headstone read simply "Baby Hope."

Baby Hope was at peace but many in the police department were dissatisfied. They'd set out to identify the little girl and bring her killer to justice. In that, they had failed but not through lack of effort. The department had committed men and resources to the case, but they were hamstrung from the start by a lack of evidence. The closest they ever got to identifying a suspect was a description by a witness who reported seeing a Hispanic man and woman dumping a blue cooler by the roadside sometime in mid-June, around the time that Baby Hope would have been killed. It got no better than that. Eventually, the investigation had to be shelved.

But the police were not yet ready to give up on the case. Baby Hope's remains were exhumed in 2006 and again in 2011, as investigators searched for DNA evidence. Then, in 2013, a new appeal was issued. Had anyone seen anything? Heard anything? Heard anyone talking about a missing or murdered child? Did anyone know of a three to five-year-old girl who had disappeared in the summer of 1991 and had not been reported as such?

Public appeals like this always bring in a deluge of calls and this one was no different. Hundreds of tips flooded in and all of these had to be investigated by the police. It would be one of the less promising leads that ultimately delivered a result. Someone had heard two women talking, one of them telling the other that her four-year-old daughter had been missing for over ten years and would be a teenager by now.

This conversation had taken place nearly two years earlier in 2011. The woman bemoaning the missing child was named Margarita Castillo. Brought in for questioning, she was asked to submit to a DNA swap. This confirmed that she was the mother of Baby Hope. Finally, the dead child had a name. She was Anjelica Castillo.

But how had the child ended up dead? Was Margarita Castillo involved? Did she know who'd killed Anjelica? Had she killed the little girl herself? Margarita vehemently denied this latter suggestion. According to her, she had never even considered Anjelica to be missing. Back in 1991, she'd been married to an abusive man named Genaro Ramirez, who was the father of her three young children. The couple had a fractious relationship and in June of that year, Genaro had walked out, taking two of the three children with him. Anjelica was one of them. Margarita had always believed that he'd taken the children back to their native Mexico. She hadn't reported the matter to the police since she and several of her family were undocumented and she'd feared deportation.

Considerable effort was now expended in finding Genaro Ramirez, considered the prime suspect in the rape and murder of his infant daughter. Those efforts would not succeed. To this day, Ramirez has not been located and has not come forward. However, the effort was not wasted. While making their inquiries, investigators learned that Genaro had taken only one of his children with him to Mexico. The other child, Anjelica, had been left in the custody of his sister, Balvina Juarez-Ramirez, in Astoria, Queens.

Just why Ramirez took one daughter with him and not the other is unclear. All we know is that, by leaving Anjelica behind, he abandoned her to a terrible fate. Living with Balvina at that time was her brother, 30-year-old Conrado Juarez, a sadistic lowlife with a taste for little girls. Did Genaro Ramirez know of his cousin's predilections when he left his daughter behind? Again, we don't know. We can only hope that he was unaware that he was handing over the child to a pedophile.

Balvina Juarez-Ramirez had passed away in the two decades since the murder of Baby Hope. She was out of the reach of justice. But Conrado Juarez was still alive, still living in New York City, working as a dishwasher at a restaurant. He was picked up there by detectives and brought in for questioning. It did not take long before he was talking, admitting to a terrible murder. The confession he gave could not have been more evil if it was scripted by the devil himself.

Angelica Castillo had suffered greatly during her short stay at the house in Astoria. She had been beaten, starved, deprived of water. She had also been sexually assaulted, raped, and sodomized by Juarez and by a friend of his. During these assaults, the child was tied to the kitchen table. According to Juarez, he had not intended to kill Anjelica but she would not stop crying while he was assaulting her and so he placed a pillow over her face and suffocated her. He and his sister then stuffed her into the cooler and transported it by cab to upper Manhattan, where they dumped it.

This entire, diabolical tale was related without a hint of remorse by the scrawny little man who was sitting across the table from the detectives. Juarez was then charged with felony murder, but he later acquired a public defender who advised him to withdraw his confession. From that point on, the narrative was that Anjelica had died after falling down the stairs and that Juarez had panicked and decided to dispose of the body, recruiting his sister to help him. Everything he'd admitted earlier had been coerced, he claimed. He was an innocent man accused of an unspeakable act.

This about turn placed prosecutors in a difficult position. Aside from Conrado Juarez's confession, they had nothing against him, no physical evidence, no witness to his depravity. Balvina Juarez-Ramirez was dead. So too was the man he'd named as participating in the rapes. Without evidence to prove his guilt, the chance was that Juarez was going to walk. Prosecutors were determined that would not happen.

The legal wrangling that ensued would continue for five years. During this time, Juarez remained charged with murder and held without bail, since he was considered a flight risk. He continued to assert his innocence even when the charges were reduced to second-degree murder. Most likely, his attorney had advised him to wait the authorities out, knowing that they'd eventually be forced to bring a weak case to trial or drop the charges and let him go.

But neither of these things would happen. Conrado Juarez would neither have his day in court nor gain his freedom. That is because Juarez had already been sentenced to death. Growing inside him was an aggressive form of pancreatic cancer. It took his life on November 19, 2018, delivering him from the human justice his evil deeds deserved. One can only hope that divine judgment was waiting for him in the afterlife.

The Accidental Detective

Rodney Denk

When Amy Weidner was just 13 years old, she had an ill-advised fling with a 17-year-old friend of her brother and ended up pregnant. At first, she tried to hide it, dressing in oversized sweaters to conceal her growing belly. Eventually, though, there was no running from the truth. Amy was forced to come clean to her mom, Gloria. She was five months pregnant at the time and determined to keep her baby. Gloria, a hard-working single mother of four, was naturally upset with her daughter's situation but nonetheless supportive. If Amy wanted to raise the child, then she would help her to do so.

And so, in October 1987, the now 14-year-old Amy Weidner welcomed her daughter into the world. She named the child Emily and was as proud as a mom could be when she brought her back to the family home on the south side of Indianapolis. Thereafter, there was a sabbatical of just six days before she returned to school. An academically gifted girl, she was determined that motherhood would not derail her education. She was convinced that she could do both.

Amy Weidner seems to have been a quite remarkable young woman. Over the next two years, she was able to successfully balance the responsibilities of motherhood with her schoolwork. During this time, she continued to bring home straight A's and made the honor roll. She was also involved in extracurricular activities, particularly the school band. On her bedside table was a glass jar, stuffed with cash she'd collected for the band through her fundraising activities. Meanwhile, Emily had grown to be a delightful two-year-old, loved and cared for by the entire Weidner clan. What had been a challenging situation had turned out very well for all concerned.

On November 13, 1989, 16-year-old Amy Weidner told her mom that she was feeling unwell and would be staying home from school. Since she seldom missed a school day, Gloria was concerned. Shortly after she arrived at her office that day, she was on the phone to check on her daughter. That call would go unanswered. So would the second and third calls Gloria placed. By the fourth failed attempt, Gloria was starting to worry. At 10 a.m., she called a neighbor and asked if she'd walk across to her house and confirm that all was well. The neighbor said that she would. About ten minutes later, she called back and said that she'd knocked at the door and gotten no response. Gloria then asked her boss if she could go home to check on her daughter.

Every terrible event that has ever happened springs from the mundane. In one moment, everything is right with the world; in the next, someone's entire universe has been turned on its head. For Gloria Weidner, all was still sane as she turned the key in the lock of her front door on that Monday morning. Surely, there must be some innocent explanation. Perhaps Amy had uncharacteristically decided to play hooky. Perhaps she'd wanted to spend the day alone with her daughter. At worst, she'd maybe gone against Gloria's wishes and taken Emily to visit her father. All of these things were going through Gloria's mind as she entered the house and called Amy's name. It was only when she reached her daughter's bedroom that the innocent explanations were swept aside. Then all that remained was nightmare reality.

Amy was lying on the bed, blood in her hair and on her face, her clothes ripped, obviously not breathing. Blood was spattered across the wall, which was also decorated with a bloody handprint. Gloria had barely a second to take this all in, to appreciate at some primal level that her daughter was beyond help. Then another thought flashed through her mind. Emily! Dashing down the hall she entered the next room, half expecting another scene of carnage. But the child was unharmed, sitting on the floor, innocently unaware that she'd just been made an orphan.

Police officers, summoned by Gloria's distressing 911 call, were soon on the scene. Here, they found Amy's lifeless body as described, battered and bruised, unmoving. The autopsy would reveal that she'd been beaten into submission before being raped and then strangled to death. The only consolation to be taken from this tragedy was that the killer had been careless. He'd left behind plenty of evidence, including a semen stain on the bedsheet and that handprint on the wall. Desperate to preserve this, crime scene technicians obtained Gloria's permission to cut out a chunk of plaster with the print on it. With this key piece of evidence, the police were confident of a quick arrest.

Right from the start, investigators were convinced of two things. The first was that the motive behind this murder was robbery. An expensive piece of stereo equipment belonging to Amy's brother had been taken. They believed that the killer had entered the residence specifically looking for this. He had not expected to find Amy at home since she was meant to be at school. It was a case of wrong place, wrong time.

All of this pointed to the second conclusion drawn by the police, that the killer was someone Amy knew. This was simple logic. If he'd entered the home looking for the stereo equipment, he must have known it was there. That meant he'd been in the house before. Also, his extreme reaction to finding Amy at home pointed to something more than a speculative break-in. Most burglars will flee when they are discovered. This one had stood his ground and committed a bloody murder. Why? Because he knew that Amy could identify him. Everything else, the rape and the theft of Amy's money jar (also missing from the house) was incidental.

Two days after her murder, Amy Weidner was laid to rest in a poignant funeral service. This was attended by several IMPD detectives who scanned the mourners, looking for anyone who might give away some clue through their actions. Thereafter, they started questioning those in Amy's inner circle, particularly friends of her brother, JP, who frequently hung out at the house. Top of their list was Tony Abercrombie, the father of Amy's child. But his hand didn't match the bloody print taken from the wall and his hair wasn't a match to samples found at the scene. The same would be true of everyone else they tested and interviewed. The case that had originally seemed like a slam dunk was slipping away.

Over the next three years, the Weidner murder inquiry remained stubbornly stalled. The police had, of course, submitted the fingerprints and DNA to various databases but the responses they got were negative. No match. Then, in 2002, they got a lead straight out of left field. A man called in to say that he'd been having dreams about Amy in which she'd provided him with details of her murder. Background checks revealed that this individual had been 16 years old and living across the street from Amy when she was killed. He had a detailed knowledge of the crime scene, which he claimed to have learned about in his dreams. The police thought otherwise. They believed they'd just caught their killer. That theory was bolstered when they learned that the suspect had been home from school on the day that Amy died.

However, this promising lead would soon fizzle out. The suspect was not a match to the physical evidence and the police subsequently learned that he had learning disabilities and other mental challenges. It was another blow to the investigation, with the files returned to gather dust among the cold case archives.

But this wasn't a case that the Indianapolis police were ready to give up on. With so much evidence in hand, they considered it solvable. In 2011, the files were handed to the department's cold case squad for another look. It was also around this time that Amy Weidner's friends and family launched a "Remember Amy" page on Facebook. It was by this quirk that Sergeant Bill Carter entered the fray.

Carter wasn't a homicide detective, nor a detective of any stripe for that matter. He was a nuisance abatement officer. His beat was policing fire code violations, building code infractions, noise complaints, underage drinking. It was through this last-named duty that he began monitoring social media channels and came to be considered somewhat of an in-house expert. When the cold case investigators needed advice on the workings of Facebook, it was Carter they turned to.

This was how Bill Carter became aware of the Weidner investigation. After reading through the case file, he became intrigued. Something about Amy's innocent young face spoke to him. It was almost as though she were asking for his help in bringing her killer to justice. And so, Carter started making inquiries, looking into the murder in his spare time. He began by going through the funeral book and through the messages on Amy's new Facebook page, looking for comments that seemed off-kilter. By this method, he eventually came up with a list of six potential suspects.

As it turned out, none of these was the man the police were looking for. But this wasn't an entirely wasted exercise. During one of the interviews that Carter conducted, someone suggested that he speak to Rodney Denk, who'd been a neighbor of the Weidners back in 1989, and a friend of Amy's brother, JP. Perhaps he'd have some information to share.

Rodney Denk had never been questioned in connection with the case before. Carter didn't know why, but he was going to set that right. He got in touch with Denk and asked if he'd be prepared to answer some questions. Denk said that he was happy to help if he could. However, he never showed for the meeting and when Carter went to check on him, he learned that Denk was gone. According to his wife, Rodney had hired a car and hit the road.

With his suspect on the run, Sgt. Carter issued a BOLO alert and then went back to the files to check the fingerprint evidence. He wondered if Rodney Denk had a criminal record and it turned out that he did. He'd been arrested for battery in 1991. That meant that his fingerprints would be on file. Carter ran a comparison to the palm print left at the crime scene. He wasn't surprised at all when it delivered a match. He had his man. Now all he had to do was find him.

Rodney Denk was eventually tracked to the house of a friend, which was quickly surrounded by police officers. Ordered to surrender, he walked out onto the porch holding a knife. "I didn't do it!" he screamed at the cops, before drawing the blade across his wrist. This wasn't a cursory cut either. It was deep and would have been fatal had help not been immediately at hand. Rushed to a nearby hospital, Denk would require surgery and a blood transfusion. By the time he was ready to talk, the police had already matched his DNA to biological material found at the crime scene.

Denial was pointless. Rodney Denk knew it and the cops knew it. Twenty-three years on from the terrible murder of Amy Weidner, her killer was finally ready to come clean. The murder had happened exactly as the original investigators had theorized. Denk had entered the Weidner residence believing that no one was home. He'd intended to steal JP's stereo but then he encountered Amy and, according to his testimony, he 'freaked out.'

It seems a significant leap from common theft to the rape and murder of an innocent young woman. Denk could provide no rational explanation for that. The court didn't need an explanation in any case, only an admission. Rodney Denk was sentenced to 65 years in prison. But for the meticulous work of an 'accidental detective,' he might have gotten away with murder.

For more True Crime books by Robert Keller

please visit:

http://bit.ly/kellerbooks

Made in United States
Orlando, FL
27 March 2024